Language Testing

Tim McNamara is Associate Professor
in the Department of Linguistics and
Applied Linguistics at the University
of Melbourne.

D0964181

Published in this series:

Oxford Introductions to Language Study

Series Editor H.G. Widdowson

Language Testing

Tim McNamara

OXFORD
UNIVERSITY PRESS

OXFORD

UNIVERSITY PRESS

Great Clarendon Street, Oxford OX2 6DP

Oxford University Press is a department of the University
of Oxford. It furthers the University's objective of excellence
in research, scholarship, and education by publishing
worldwide in

Oxford New York

Athens Auckland Bangkok Bogotá Buenos Aires
Calcutta Cape Town Chennai Dar es Salaam Delhi
Florence Hong Kong Istanbul Karachi Kuala Lumpur
Madrid Melbourne Mexico City Mumbai Nairobi Paris
São Paulo Singapore Taipei Tokyo Toronto Warsaw

with associated companies in Berlin Ibadan

OXFORD and OXFORDENGLISH are registered trade marks of
Oxford University Press in the UK and in certain other countries

ISBN 0 19 437222 7

2000 Impression

Printed in Hong Kong

To Terry Quinn

Contents

Preface

Purpose

What justification might there be for a series of introductions to language study? After all, linguistics is already well served with introductory texts: expositions and explanations which are comprehensive, authoritative, and excellent in their way. Generally speaking, however, their way is the essentially academic one of providing a detailed initiation into the discipline of linguistics, and they tend to be lengthy and technical: appropriately so, given their purpose. But they can be quite daunting to the novice. There is also a need for a more general and gradual introduction to language: transitional texts which will ease people into an understanding of complex ideas. This series of introductions is designed to serve this need.

Their purpose, therefore, is not to supplant but to support the more academically oriented introductions to linguistics: to prepare the conceptual ground. They are based on the belief that it is an advantage to have a broad map of the terrain sketched out before one considers its more specific features on a smaller scale, a general context in reference to which the detail makes sense. It is sometimes the case that students are introduced to detail without it being made clear what it is a detail of. Clearly, a general understanding of ideas is not sufficient: there needs to be closer scrutiny. But equally, close scrutiny can be myopic and meaningless unless it is related to the larger view. Indeed it can be said that the precondition of more particular enquiry is an awareness of what, in general, the particulars are about. This series is designed to provide this large-scale view of different areas of language study. As such it can serve as preliminary to (and precondition for) the more specific and specialized enquiry which students of linguistics are required to undertake.

But the series is not only intended to be helpful to such students. There are many people who take an interest in language without being academically engaged in linguistics per se. Such people may recognize the importance of understanding language for their own lines of enquiry, or for their own practical purposes, or quite simply for making them aware of something which figures so centrally in their everyday lives. If linguistics has revealing and relevant things to say about language, this should presumably not be a privileged revelation, but one accessible to people other than linguists. These books have been so designed as to accommodate these broader interests too: they are meant to be introductions to language more generally as well as to linguistics as a discipline.

Design

The books in the series are all cut to the same basic pattern. There are four parts: Survey, Readings, References, and Glossary.

Survey

This is a summary overview of the main features of the area of language study concerned: its scope and principles of enquiry, its basic concerns and key concepts. These are expressed and explained in ways which are intended to make them as accessible as possible to people who have no prior knowledge or expertise in the subject. The Survey is written to be readable and is uncluttered by the customary scholarly references. In this sense, it is simple. But it is not simplistic. Lack of specialist expertise does not imply an inability to understand or evaluate ideas. Ignorance means lack of knowledge, not lack of intelligence. The Survey, therefore, is meant to be challenging. It draws a map of the subject area in such a way as to stimulate thought and to invite a critical participation in the exploration of ideas. This kind of conceptual cartography has its dangers of course: the selection of what is significant, and the manner of its representation, will not be to the liking of everybody, particularly not, perhaps, to some of those inside the discipline. But these surveys are written in the belief that there must be an alternative to a technical account on the one hand, and an idiot's guide on the other if linguistics is to be made relevant to people in the wider world.

Readings

Some people will be content to read, and perhaps re-read, the summary Survey. Others will want to pursue the subject and so will use the Survey as the preliminary for more detailed study. The Readings provide the necessary transition. For here the reader is presented with texts extracted from the specialist literature. The purpose of these Readings is quite different from the Survey. It is to get readers to focus on the specifics of what is said, and how it is said, in these source texts. Questions are provided to further this purpose: they are designed to direct attention to points in each text, how they compare across texts, and how they deal with the issues discussed in the Survey. The idea is to give readers an initial familiarity with the more specialist idiom of the linguistics literature, where the issues might not be so readily accessible, and to encourage them into close critical reading.

References

One way of moving into more detailed study is through the Readings. Another is through the annotated References in the third section of each book. Here there is a selection of works (books and articles) for further reading. Accompanying comments indicate how these deal in more detail with the issues discussed in the different chapters of the Survey.

Glossary

Certain terms in the Survey appear in bold. These are terms used in a special or technical sense in the discipline. Their meanings are made clear in the discussion, but they are also explained in the Glossary at the end of each book. The Glossary is cross-referenced to the Survey, and therefore serves at the same time as an index. This enables readers to locate the term and what it signifies in the more general discussion, thereby, in effect, using the Survey as a summary work of reference.

Use

The series has been designed so as to be flexible in use. Each title is separate and self-contained, with only the basic format in common. The four sections of the format, as described here, can be drawn upon and combined in different ways, as required by the needs, or interests, of different readers. Some may be content with the Survey and the Glossary and may not want to follow up the suggested References. Some may not wish to venture into the Readings. Again, the Survey might be considered as appropriate preliminary reading for a course in applied linguistics or teacher education, and the Readings more appropriate for seminar discussion during the course. In short, the notion of an introduction will mean different things to different people, but in all cases the concern is to provide access to specialist knowledge and stimulate an awareness of its significance. This series as a whole has been designed to provide this access and promote this awareness in respect to different areas of language study.

H. G. WIDDOWSON

Author's acknowledgements

Language testing is often thought of as an arcane and difficult field, and politically incorrect to boot. The opportunity to provide an introduction to the conceptual interest of the field and to some of its procedures has been an exciting one. The immediate genesis for this book came from an invitation from Henry Widdowson, who proved to be an illuminating and supportive editor throughout the process of the book's writing. It was an honour and a pleasure to work with him.

The real origins of the book lay further back, when over 15 years ago Terry Quinn of the University of Melbourne urged me to take up a consultancy on language testing at the Australian Language Centre in Jakarta. Terry has been an invaluable support and mentor throughout my career in applied linguistics, nowhere more so than in the field of language testing, which in his usual clear-sighted way he has always understood as being inherently political and social in character, a perspective which I am only now, after twelve years of research in the area, beginning to properly understand. I am also grateful to my other principal teachers about language testing, Alan Davies, Lyle Bachman, and Bernard Spolsky, and to my friend and colleague Elana Shohamy, from whom I have learnt so much in conversations long into the night about these and other matters. I also owe a deep debt to Sally Jacoby, a challenging thinker and great teacher, who has helped me frame and contextualize in new ways my work in this field. My colleagues at Melbourne, Brian Lynch and Alastair Pennycook, have dragged me kicking and screaming at least some way into the postmodern era. The Language Testing Research Centre at the University of Melbourne has been for over a decade the perfect environment within which thinking on language testing can flourish, and I am grateful to (again) Alan Davies and to Cathie Elder, and to all my other colleagues there. Whatever clarity the book may have is principally due to my dear friend and soulmate Lillian Nativ, who remains the most difficult and critical student I have had. Being a wonderful teacher herself she will never accept anything less than clear explanations. The students to whom I have taught language testing or whose research I have supervised over the years have also shaped this book in considerable ways. At OUP, I have had excellent help from Julia Sallabank and Belinda Fenn.

On a more personal note I am grateful for the continuing support and friendship of Marie-Thérèse Jensen and the love of our son Daniel.

TIM MCNAMARA

Survey

1

Testing, testing …
What is a language test?

Testing is a universal feature of social life. Throughout history people have been put to the test to prove their capabilities or to establish their credentials; this is the stuff of Homeric epic, of Arthurian legend. In modern societies such tests have proliferated rapidly. Testing for purposes of detection or to establish identity has become an accepted part of sport (drugs testing), the law (DNA tests, paternity tests, lie detection tests), medicine (blood tests, cancer screening tests, hearing, and eye tests), and other fields. Tests to see how a person performs particularly in relation to a threshold of performance have become important social institutions and fulfil a gatekeeping function in that they control entry to many important social roles. These include the driving test and a range of tests in education and the workplace. Given the centrality of testing in social life, it is perhaps surprising that its practice is so little understood. In fact, as so often happens in the modern world, this process, which so much affects our lives, becomes the province of experts and we become dependent on them. The expertise of those involved in testing is seen as remote and obscure, and the tests they produce are typically associated in us with feelings of anxiety and powerlessness.

What is true of testing in general is true also of language testing, not a topic likely to quicken the pulse or excite much immediate interest. If it evokes any reaction, it will probably take the form of negative associations. For many, language tests may conjure up an image of an examination room, a test paper with questions, desperate scribbling against the clock. Or a chair outside the interview room and a nervous victim waiting with rehearsed phrases to be called into an inquisitional conversation with the examiners. But there is more to language testing than this.

To begin with, the very nature of testing has changed quite radically over the years to become less impositional, more humanistic, conceived not so much to catch people out on what they do not know, but as a more neutral assessment of what they do. Newer forms of language assessment may no longer involve the ordeal of a single test performance under time constraints. Learners may be required to build up a portfolio of written or recorded oral performances for assessment. They may be observed in their normal activities of communication in the language classroom on routine pedagogical tasks. They may be asked to carry out activities outside the classroom context and provide evidence of their performance. Pairs of learners may be asked to take part in role plays or in group discussions as part of oral assessment. Tests may be delivered by computer, which may tailor the form of the test to the particular abilities of individual candidates. Learners may be encouraged to assess aspects of their own abilities.

Clearly these assessment activities are very different from the solitary confinement and interrogation associated with traditional testing. The question arises, of course, as to how these different activities have developed, and what their principles of design might be. It is the purpose of this book to address these questions.

Understanding language testing

There are many reasons for developing a critical understanding of the principles and practice of language assessment. Obviously you will need to do so if you are actually responsible for language test development and claim expertise in this field. But many other people working in the field of language study more generally will want to be able to participate as necessary in the discourse of this field, for a number of reasons.

First, language tests play a powerful role in many people's lives, acting as gateways at important transitional moments in education, in employment, and in moving from one country to another. Since language tests are devices for the institutional control of individuals, it is clearly important that they should be understood, and subjected to scrutiny. Secondly, you may be working with language tests in your professional life as a teacher or administrator, teaching to a test, administering tests, or relying on information from tests to make decisions on the placement of students on particular courses.

Finally, if you are conducting research in language study you may need to have measures of the language proficiency of your subjects. For this you need either to choose an appropriate existing language test or design your own.

Thus, an understanding of language testing is relevant both for those actually involved in creating language tests, and also more generally for those involved in using tests or the information they provide, in practical and research contexts.

Types of test

Not all language tests are of the same kind. They differ with respect to how they are designed, and what they are for: in other words, in respect to test *method* and test *purpose*.

In terms of method, we can broadly distinguish traditional **paper-and-pencil language tests** from **performance tests**. Paper-and-pencil tests take the form of the familiar examination question paper. They are typically used for the assessment either of separate components of language knowledge (grammar, vocabulary etc.) or of receptive understanding (listening and reading comprehension). **Test items** in such tests, particularly if they are professionally made standardized tests, will often be in **fixed response format** in which a number of possible responses is presented from which the candidate is required to choose. There are several types of fixed response format, of which the most important is **multiple choice format**, as in the following example from a vocabulary test:

Select the most appropriate completion of the sentence.

> *I wonder what the newspaper says about the new play. I must read the*
> (a) *criticism*
> (b) *opinion*
> *(c) *review*
> (d) *critic*

Items in multiple choice format present a range of anticipated likely responses to the test-taker. Only one of the presented alternatives (the *key*, marked here with an asterisk) is correct; the others (the *distractors*) are based on typical confusions or misunderstandings seen in learners' attempts to answer the questions freely in try-outs of the test material, or on observation of errors made in the process of learning more generally. The candidate's task is simply to choose the best alternative among those presented. Scoring then follows automatically, and is indeed often done by machine. Such tests are thus efficient to administer and score, but since they only require picking out one item from a set of given alternatives, they are not much use in testing the productive skills of speaking and writing, except indirectly.

In performance based tests, language skills are assessed in an act of communication. Performance tests are most commonly tests of speaking and writing, in which a more or less extended sample of speech or writing is elicited from the test-taker, and judged by one or more trained **raters** using an agreed **rating procedure**. These samples are elicited in the context of simulations of real-world tasks in realistic contexts.

Test purpose

Language tests also differ according to their *purpose*. In fact, the same form of test may be used for differing purposes, although in other cases the purpose may affect the form. The most familiar distinction in terms of test purpose is that between **achievement** and **proficiency tests**.

Achievement tests are associated with the process of instruction. Examples would be: end of course tests, portfolio assessments, or observational procedures for recording progress on the basis of classroom work and participation. Achievement tests accumulate evidence during, or at the end of, a course of study in order to see whether and where progress has been made in terms of the goals of learning. Achievement tests should support the teaching to which they relate. Writers have been critical of the use of multiple choice standardized tests for this purpose, saying that they have a negative effect on classrooms as teachers teach to the test, and that there is often a mismatch between the test and the curriculum, for example where the latter emphasizes performance. An achievement test may be self-enclosed in the sense that it may not bear any direct relationship to language use in the world outside the classroom (it may focus on knowledge of particular points of grammar or vocabulary, for example). This will not be the case if the syllabus is itself concerned with the outside world, as the test will then automatically reflect that reality in the process of reflecting the syllabus. More commonly though, achievement tests are more easily able to be innovative, and to reflect progressive aspects of the curriculum, and are associated with some of the most interesting new developments in language assessment in the movement known as **alternative assessment**. This approach stresses the need for assessment to be integrated with the goals of the curriculum and to have a constructive relationship with teaching and learning. Standardized tests are seen as too often having a negative, restricting influence on progressive teaching. Instead, for example, learners may be encouraged to share in the responsibility for assessment, and be trained to evaluate their own capacities in performance in a range of settings in a process known as **self-assessment**.

Whereas achievement tests relate to the past in that they measure what language the students have learned as a result of teaching, *proficiency tests* look to the future situation of language use without necessarily any reference to the previous process of teaching. The future 'real life' language use is referred to as the **criterion**. In recent years tests have increasingly sought to include performance features in their design, whereby characteristics of the criterion setting are represented. For example, a test of the communicative abilities of health professionals in work settings will be based on representations of such workplace tasks as communicating with patients or other health professionals. Courses of study to prepare candidates for the test may grow up in the wake of its establishment, particularly if it has an important gate-keeping function, for example admission to an overseas university, or to an occupation requiring practical second language skills.

The criterion

Testing is about making inferences; this essential point is obscured by the fact that some testing procedures, particularly in performance assessment, appear to involve direct observation. Even where the test simulates real world behaviour—reading a newspaper, role playing a conversation with a patient, listening to a lecture—test performances are not valued in themselves, but only as indicators of how a person would perform similar, or related, tasks in the real world setting of interest. Understanding testing involves recognizing a distinction between the *criterion* (relevant communicative behaviour in the target situation) and the *test*. The distinction between test and criterion is set out for performance-based tests in Figure 1.1

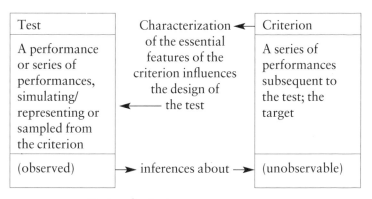

FIGURE 1.1 *Test and criterion*

Test performances are used as the basis for making inferences about criterion performances. Thus, for example, listening to a lecture in a test is used to infer how a person would cope with listening to lectures in the course of study he/she is aiming to enter. It is important to stress that although this criterion behaviour, as relevant to the appropriate communicative role (as nurse, for example, or student), is the real object of interest, it cannot be accounted for as such by the test. It remains elusive since it cannot be directly observed.

There has been a resistance among some proponents of **direct testing** to this idea. Surely test tasks can be authentic samples of behaviour? Sometimes it is true that the materials and tasks in language tests can be relatively realistic but they can never be *real*. For example, an oral examination might include a conversation, or a role-play appropriate to the target destination. In a test of English for immigrant health professionals, this might be between a doctor and a patient. But even where performance test materials appear to be very realistic compared to traditional paper-and-pencil tests, it is clear that the test performance does not exist for its own sake. The test-taker is not really reading the newspaper provided in the test for the specific information within it; the test taking doctor is not really advising the 'patient'. As one writer famously put it, everyone is aware that in a conversation used to assess oral ability 'this is a test, not a tea party'. The effect of test method on the realism of tests will be discussed further in Chapter 3.

There are a number of other limits to the **authenticity** of tests, which force us to recognize an inevitable gap between the test and the criterion. For one thing, even in those forms of direct performance assessment where the period in which behaviour is observed is quite extended (for example, a teacher's ability to use the target language in class may be observed on a series of lessons with real students), there comes a point at which we have to stop observing and reach our decision about the candidate—that is, make an inference about the candidate's probable behaviour in situations subsequent to the assessment period. While it may be likely that our conclusions based on the assessed lessons may be valid in relation to the subsequent unobserved teaching, differences in the conditions of performance may in fact jeopardize their **validity** (their generalizability). For example, factors such as the careful preparation of lessons when the teacher was under observation may not be replicated in the criterion, and the effect of this cannot be known in advance. The point is that observation of behaviour as part of the activity of assessment is naturally self-limiting, on logistical grounds if for no other reason. In fact, of course, most test situations allow only a very brief period of sampling of candidate behaviour—usually a couple of hours or so at most; oral tests may last only a few minutes. Another constraint on direct knowledge of the criterion is the testing equivalent of the Observer's Paradox: that is, the very act of observation may change the behaviour being observed. We all know how tense being assessed can make us, and conversely how easy it sometimes is to play to the camera, or the gallery.

In judging test performances then, we are not interested in the observed instances of actual use for their own sake; if we were, and that is all we were interested in, the sample performance would not be a test. Rather, we want to know what the particular performance reveals of the potential for subsequent performances in the criterion situation. We look so to speak underneath or through the test performance to those qualities in it which are indicative of what is held to underlie it.

If our inferences about subsequent candidate behaviour are wrong, this may have serious consequences for the candidate and others who have a stake in the decision. Investigating the defensibility of the inferences about candidates that have been made on the basis of test performance is known as **test validation**, and is the main focus of testing research.

The test–criterion relationship

The very practical activity of testing is inevitably underpinned by theoretical understanding of the relationship between the criterion and test performance. Tests are based on theories of the nature of language use in the target setting and the way in which this is understood will be reflected in test design. Theories of language and language in use have of course developed in very different directions over the years and tests will reflect a variety of theoretical orientations. For example, approaches which see performance in the criterion as an essentially cognitive activity will understand language use in terms of cognitive constructs such as knowledge, ability, and proficiency. On the other hand, approaches which conceive of criterion performance as a social and interactional achievement will emphasize social roles and interaction in test design. This will be explored in detail in Chapter 2.

However, it is not enough simply to accept the proposed relationship between criterion and test implicit in all test design. Testers need to check the empirical evidence for their position in the light of candidates' actual performance on test tasks. In other words, analysis of test data is called for, to put the theory of the test–criterion relationship itself to the test. For example, current models of communicative ability state that there are distinct aspects of that ability, which should be measured in tests. As a result, raters of speaking skills are sometimes required to fill in a grid where they record separate impressions of aspects of speaking such as pronunciation, appropriateness, grammatical accuracy, and the like. Using data (test scores) produced by such procedures, we will be in a position to examine empirically the relationship between scores given under the various categories. Are the categories indeed independent? Test validation thus involves two things. In the first place, it involves understanding how, in principle, performance on the test can be used to infer performance in the criterion. In the second place, it involves using empirical data from test performances to investigate the defensibility of that understanding and hence of the interpretations (the judgements about test-takers) that follow from it. These matters will be considered in detail in Chapter 5, on test validity.

Conclusion

In this chapter we have looked at the nature of the test–criterion relationship. We have seen that a language test is a procedure for gathering evidence of general or specific language abilities from performance on tasks designed to provide a basis for predictions about an individual's use of those abilities in real world contexts. All such tests require us to make a distinction between the *data* of the learner's behaviour, the actual language that is produced in test performance, and what these data signify, that is to say what they count as in terms of *evidence* of 'proficiency', 'readiness for communicative roles in the real world', and so on. Testing thus necessarily involves interpretation of the data of test performance as evidence of knowledge or ability of one kind or another. Like the soothsayers of ancient Rome, who inspected the entrails of slain animals in order to make their interpretations and subsequent predictions of future events, testers need specialized knowledge of what signs to look for, and a theory of the relationship of those signs to events in the world. While language testing resembles other kinds of testing in that it conforms to general principles and practices of measurement, as other areas of testing do, it is distinctive in that the signs and evidence it deals with have to do specifically with language. We need then to consider how views about the nature of language have had an impact on test design.

2
Communication and the design of language tests

Essential to the activities of designing tests and interpreting the meaning of test scores is the view of language and language use embodied in the test. The term **test construct** refers to those aspects of knowledge or skill possessed by the candidate which are being measured. Although this term is taken from psychology, we should note that the knowledge or skill being assessed does not have to be defined in psychological terms. Thus some scholars have taken a social rather than psychological view of language performance and would define the test construct accordingly. Defining the test construct involves being clear about what knowledge of language consists of, and how that knowledge is deployed in actual performance (language use). Understanding what view the test takes of language use in the criterion is necessary for determining the link between test and criterion in performance testing. This is not just an academic matter. It has important practical implications, because according to what view the test takes, the 'look' of the test will be different, reporting of scores will change, and test performance will be interpreted differently. The difference of format between paper-and-pencil tests and performance tests is not just incidental; it reflects an implicit difference between views of language and language use.

Discrete point tests

Early theories of test performance, influenced by structuralist linguistics, saw knowledge of language as consisting of mastery of the features of the language as a system. This position was clearly articulated by Robert Lado in his highly influential book *Language Testing*, published in 1961. Testing focused on candidates' knowledge of the grammatical system, of vocabulary, and of aspects of pronunciation. There was a tendency to atomize and decontextualize the knowledge to be tested, and to test aspects of knowledge in isolation. Thus, the points of grammar chosen for assessment would be tested one at a time; and tests of grammar would be separate from tests of vocabulary. Material to be tested was presented with minimal context, for example in an isolated sentence. This practice of testing separate, individual points of knowledge, known as **discrete point testing**, was reinforced by theory and practice within **psychometrics**, the emerging science of the measurement of cognitive abilities. This stressed the need for certain properties of measurement, particularly reliability, or consistency of estimation of candidates' abilities. It was found that this could be best achieved through constructing a test consisting of many small items all directed at the same general target—say, grammatical structure, or vocabulary knowledge. In order to test these individual points, item formats of the multiple choice question type were most suitable. While there was also realization among some writers that the integrated nature of performance needed to be reflected somewhere in a test battery, the usual way of handling this integration was at the level of **skills testing**, so that the four language macroskills of listening, reading, writing, and speaking were in various degrees tested (again, in strict isolation from one another) as a supplement to discrete point tests. This period of language testing has been called the psychometric-structuralist period and was in its heyday in the 1960s; but the practices adopted at that time have remained hugely influential.

Integrative and pragmatic tests

Within a decade, the necessity of assessing the practical language skills of foreign students wishing to study at universities in Britain and the US, together with the need within the communicative movement in teaching for tests which measured productive capacities for language, led to a demand for language tests which involved an integrated performance on the part of the language user. The discrete point tradition of testing was seen as focusing too exclusively on knowledge of the formal linguistic system for its own sake rather than on the way such knowledge is used to achieve communication. The new orientation resulted in the development of tests which integrated knowledge of relevant systematic features of language (pronunciation, grammar, vocabulary) with an understanding of context. As a result, a distinction was drawn between discrete point tests and **integrative tests** such as speaking in oral interviews, the composing of whole written texts, and tests involving comprehension of extended discourse (both spoken and written). The problem was that such integrative tests tended to be expensive, as they were time consuming and difficult to score, requiring trained raters; and in any case were potentially unreliable (that is, where judges were involved, the judges would disagree).

Research carried out by the American, John Oller, in the 1970s seemed to offer a solution. Oller offered a new view of language and language use underpinning tests, focusing less on knowledge of language and more on the psycholinguistic processing involved in language use. Language use was seen as involving two factors: (1) the on-line processing of language in real time (for example, in naturalistic speaking and listening activities), and (2) a 'pragmatic mapping' component, that is, the way formal knowledge of the systematic features of language was drawn on for the expression and understanding of meaning in context. A test of language use had to involve both of these features, neither of which was felt to be captured in the discrete point tradition of testing. Further, Oller proposed what came to be known as the **Unitary Competence Hypothesis**, that is, that performance on a whole range of tests (which he termed **pragmatic tests**) depended on the same underlying capacity in the learner—the ability to integrate grammatical, lexical, contextual, and pragmatic knowledge in test performance. He argued that certain kinds of more economical and efficient tests, particularly the **cloze test** (a gap-filling reading test), measured the same kinds of skills as those tested in productive tests of the types listed above. It was argued that a cloze test was an appropriate substitute for a test of productive skills because it required readers to integrate grammatical, lexical, contextual, and pragmatic knowledge in order to be able to supply the missing words. A cloze test was a reading test, consisting of a text of approximately 400 words in length. After an introductory sentence or two which was left intact, words were systematically removed—

every 5th, 6th or 7th word was a typical procedure—and replaced with a blank. The task was for the reader to supply the missing word. Various scoring methods (exact word replacement, any acceptable word replacement) were tried out and seemed to provide much the same information about the relative abilities of readers. Such tests were easy to construct, relatively easy to score, were based on a compelling theory of language use, and seemed an attractive alternative to more elaborate and expensive tests of the productive skills of speaking and writing. The cloze thus became a very popular form of test in the 1970s and early 1980s (and is still widely used today).

Unfortunately, further work soon showed that cloze tests on the whole seemed mostly to be measuring the same kinds of things as discrete point tests of grammar and vocabulary. It seems that there are no short cuts in the testing of communicative skills.

Communicative language tests

From the early 1970s, a new theory of language and language use began to exert a significant influence on language teaching and potentially on language testing. This was Hymes's theory of communicative competence, which greatly expanded the scope of what was covered by an understanding of language and the ability to use language in context, particularly in terms of the social demands of performance. Hymes saw that knowing a language was more than knowing its rules of grammar. There were culturally specific rules of use which related the language used to features of the communicative context. For example, ways of speaking or writing appropriate to communication with close friends may not be the same as those used in communicating with strangers, or in professional contexts. Although the relevance of Hymes's theory to language testing was recognized more or less immediately on its appearance, it took a decade for its actual impact on practice to be felt, in the development of communicative language tests. Communicative language tests ultimately came to have two features:

1 They were performance tests, requiring assessment to be carried out when the learner or candidate was engaged in an extended act of communication, either receptive or productive, or both.

2 They paid attention to the social roles candidates were likely to assume in real world settings, and offered a means of specifying the demands of such roles in detail.

The second of these features distinguishes communicative language tests from the integrative/pragmatic testing tradition. The theory of communicative competence represented a profound shift from a psychological perspective on language, which sees language as an internal phenomenon, to a sociological one, focusing on the external, social functions of language.

Developments in Britain were particularly significant. The Royal Society of Arts developed influential examinations in English as a Foreign Language with innovative features such as the use of authentic texts and real world tasks; and the British Council and other authorities developed communicative tests of English as a Foreign Language for overseas students intending to study at British universities. These latter tests in some cases involved careful study of the communicative roles and tasks facing such students in Britain as the basis for test design; this stage of the process is known as a **job analysis**. This approach has continued to be used in the development of tests in occupational settings. For example, in the development of an Australian test of English as a second language for health professionals, those familiar with clinical situations in hospital settings were surveyed, and tasks such as communicating with patients, presenting cases to colleagues, and so on were identified and ranked according to criteria such as complexity, frequency, and importance as the basis for subsequent test task design. Test materials were then developed to simulate such roles and tasks where possible.

Models of communicative ability

The practical and imaginative response to the challenge of communicative language testing was matched by a continuing theoretical engagement with the idea of communicative competence and its implications for the performance requirement of communicative language testing. Various writers have tried to specify the components of communicative competence in second languages and their role in performance. This has been done in order to provide a comprehensive framework for test development and testing research, and a basis for the interpretation of test performance.

In their first form, such models specified the components of knowledge of language without dealing in detail with their role in performance. Various aspects of knowledge or competence were specified in the early 1980s by Michael Canale and Merrill Swain in Canada:

1 *grammatical* or formal competence, which covered the kind of knowledge (of systematic features of grammar, lexis, and phonology) familiar from the discrete point tradition of testing;

2 *sociolinguistic* competence, or knowledge of rules of language use in terms of what is appropriate to different types of interlocutors, in different settings, and on different topics;

3 *strategic* competence, or the ability to compensate in performance for incomplete or imperfect linguistic resources in a second language; and

4 *discourse* competence, or the ability to deal with extended use of language in context.

Note that strategic competence is oddly named as it is not a type of stored knowledge, as the first two aspects of competence appear to be, but a capacity for strategic behaviour in performance, which is likely to involve non-cognitive issues such as confidence, preparedness to take risks, and so on. Discourse competence similarly has elements of a general intellectual flexibility in negotiating meaning in discourse, in addition to a stored knowledge aspect—in this case, knowledge of the way in which links between different sentences or ideas in a text are explicitly marked, through the use of pronouns, conjunctions, and the like.

Further years of discussion and reflection on this framework have led to its more detailed reformulation. There has, to begin with, been a further specification of different components of knowledge that would appear to be included in communicative competence. Thus Lyle Bachman, for example, has identified subcategories of knowledge within the broader categories of grammatical, discourse, and sociolinguistic competencies. At the same time, strategic competence no longer features as a component of such knowledge. In fact, the notion of strategic competence remains crucial in understanding second language performance, but it has been reconceptualized. Instead of referring to a compensatory strategy for learners, it is seen as a more general phenomenon of language use. In this view, strategic competence is understood as a general reasoning ability which enables one to negotiate meaning in context.

This reworking of the idea of strategic competence has important implications for assessment. If strategic competence is not part of language knowledge, yet does have an impact on performance, should it be included as part of the focus of assessment? After all, competent native speakers differ in their conversational facility and their preparedness to take risks in communication, and these differences of temperament rather than competence are likely to carry over into second language communication. If we are to judge strategic competence, by what standards should we do so, given the variability among native speakers in this regard? On the other hand, if we are to exclude strategic competence as a target of assessment, how can we equalize its impact on impressions of performance? In other words, what at first look like abstract theoretical debates about the nature of competence and performance in language tests have very practical consequences for test design and for the procedures by which judges will make ratings of performance.

Apart from the increasing specification of what knowledge is presupposed in communication, there has also been an attempt to grasp the slippery issue of what things other than knowledge are called upon in performance in communicative tests, particularly where performances involve interaction with another person, as in oral performance tests. These will include confidence, motivation, emotional states, the identities of candidate and interlocutor, and so on. Of course, an awareness of the complexity of factors involved in performance complicates enormously the task of standardizing the conditions of assessment (in the interest of fairness). The slowness with which the field has come to grips with the issues involved is perhaps motivated by a reluctance to face the difficulties of achieving a fair assessment in performance tests.

Another development has been the attempt to characterize the real world tasks in the criterion situation identified through job analysis in terms of the aspects of ability or skill (as specified in the model of ability) they call upon. This has involved the analysis of tasks in terms of those components of knowledge that they require, so that performance on tasks can be used as evidence of command (or otherwise) of specific components of knowledge and skill. In this way the content of test tasks and test method are specified more precisely and this can provide a more explicit basis for claims to the validity of interpretations of test performance.

It should be noted that the approach to thinking about communicative language ability in terms of discrete components leaves us with aspects of language analysed out as distinct and unrelated. There is still therefore the problem, which models of communicative competence were designed to resolve, of how to account for the way the different aspects act upon each other in actual communication. Paradoxically, as models of communicative competence become more analytic, so they take us back to the problems of discrete point testing usually associated with testing of form alone.

Nevertheless, the elaboration of models of abilities underlying performance has been helpful for both mapping research in language testing and classifying language tests, and providing language test developers and researchers with a common language to talk about the focus of their work. And even though the modelling of communicative language ability may appear somewhat dauntingly complex and even abstract at times, the issues being considered in this debate have very clear practical consequences as we have seen.

But it is also true that attempts to apply a complex framework for modelling communicative language ability directly in test design have not always proved easy, mainly because of the complexity of the framework. This has sometimes resulted in a rather tokenistic acknowledgement of the framework and then a disregard for it at the stage of practical test design. Where a more thorough attempt to base test design on the framework has been made, the procedures for specifying test content prove to be unwieldy.

If communicative tests are to move forward they will need to address the problem of feature isolation raised earlier, whereby features of language use are analysed out and performance necessarily distorted because performance is not a collection of features but an integrated interplay between them. The issue raised here takes us back to the points made previously, in Chapter 1, that criterion behaviour is bound to be elusive and in principle beyond the scope of assessment in a direct sense. A further issue involves the implications for test validity of interpreting test performance, for example on a speaking test, in terms of only one of the participants, the candidate. Clearly, many others than the candidate affect the chances of the candidate achieving a successful score for the performance. These will include those who frame the opportunity for performance at the test design stage; those with whom the candidate interacts; those who rate the performance; and those responsible for designing and managing the rating procedure. Instead of focusing on the candidate in isolation, the candidate's performance needs to be seen and evaluated as part of a joint construction by a number of participants, including interlocutors, test designers, and raters. The intrinsically social character of test performance is discussed at length in Chapter 7.

Conclusion

In this chapter we have examined a number of influential 'schools' of language testing, the latter ones claiming to supersede the earlier ones on the grounds of the advances they have made in understanding the essential nature of performance (language use) in the criterion. In fact, the testing practices associated with earlier approaches have far from disappeared, which is why appreciating earlier work is necessary for understanding the current rather eclectic scene in language testing.

Historically, views of performance in the criterion situation have focused either on the cognitive abilities that the individual brings to it or on its social character. Attempts have also been made to resolve the inevitable difference between these perspectives. The ability to participate in the social nature of interaction is seen as depending on the candidate knowing certain socially determined communicative conventions, for example, how to match the form of language to the topic, the setting, the interlocutor, and so on. In this way, an understanding of the social character of the criterion setting is formulated in terms of relevant knowledge of socially determined communicative conventions. The social dimension of communication then becomes part of what the candidate needs to know, and can thus be part of the cognitive dimensions of successful performance. Although all tests imply a view of the nature of the criterion, these views are not always explicit in testing schemes.

3
The testing cycle

Designing and introducing a new test is a little like getting a new car on the road. It involves a design stage, a construction stage, and a try-out stage before the test is finally operational. But that suggests a linear process, whereas in fact test development involves a cycle of activity, because the actual operational use of the test generates evidence about its own qualities. We need to pay attention to this information, indeed actively to seek it out, and use it to do further thinking about the test—and so another turn of the cycle begins.

In this chapter we will outline the stages and typical procedures in this cyclical process. Further details about some of the stages will be given in subsequent chapters.

Who starts the circle turning? New situations arise, usually associated with social or political changes, which generate the need for a new test or assessment procedure. These include the growth of international education, increased labour flows between countries as the result of treaties, the educational impact of immigration or refugee programmes, school curriculum reform, or reform of vocational education, and training for adults in the light of technological change. For example, the needs of the US Government during the Cold War for personnel who could handle spoken communication in a range of strategically important languages inspired one of the most forward-looking developments in language testing, the **Oral Proficiency Interview** (**OPI**). In this procedure, performance in a short interaction with a native speaker interlocutor is judged against a set of descriptions of performance at various levels. With various modifications, this has remained the most commonly used means for the direct testing of spoken language skills. The political and social origins and meaning of language tests have recently been brought more clearly into focus, and the complex responsibilities of the language tester as the agent of political, commercial, and bureaucratic forces are the subject of discussion in Chapter 7.

Those responsible for managing the implications of change, usually in corporations or bureaucracies, commission the work of test developers. When school systems are involved, the work of responding to changing needs is met from within education ministries, often with the assistance of university researchers. But particularly with the assessment of adults, or where assessment involves international contexts, testing agencies with specialist expertise in language testing become involved. Such agencies are responsible for the two major tests used to measure the English of international students wishing to study in universities in the English-speaking world: the American **Test of English as a Foreign Language** (**TOEFL**) and the British/Australian **International English Language Testing System** (**IELTS**).

Understanding the constraints

Before they begin thinking in detail about the design of a test, test developers will need to get the lay of the land, that is, to establish the constraints under which they are working, and under which the test will be administered. What resources, physical and financial, are available for test development and test operation? There is no point in proposing a performance test if there is no money available for the provision of properly trained raters, or if the provision of trained raters cannot be guaranteed in certain remote locations in which the test is to be administered. Tests of speaking and listening delivered in language laboratories, or tests delivered via computer, are not practical options where the technology is not available. **Test security** is also a constraint—can we be sure that detailed knowledge of the contents of any version will be kept from candidates until the time of the examination? The functions that any assessment procedure are required to perform can also act as an important constraint. For example, there is an increasing tendency for governments to require the reporting of the success of language programmes against national scales or benchmarks. This may mean that any procedure that teachers use in their classrooms to gather information on the progress of learners

may have to be compatible with such over-arching reporting schemes.

Following this initial ground-clearing, we move on to the detailed design of the test. This will involve procedures to establish **test content**, what the test contains and **test method**, the way in which it will appear to the test-taker, the format in which responses will be required, and how these responses will be scored.

Test content

From a practical point of view test design begins with decisions about test content, what will go into the test. In fact, these decisions imply a view of the test construct, the way language and language use in test performance are seen, together with the relationship of test performance to real-world contexts of use. In the previous chapter, we explored a number of current approaches to thinking about test constructs. In major test projects, articulating and defining the test construct may be the first stage of test development, resulting in an elaborated statement of the theoretical framework for the test. Even here constraints can operate; the new test may have to fit into an approach which has been determined in advance, for example by educational policy makers. This is currently the case in assessment which takes place as part of vocational training, where the approach to training will determine the approach to assessment; this is discussed further in Chapter 7 on the institutional character of language tests.

Establishing test content involves careful sampling from the **domain** of the test, that is, the set of tasks or the kinds of behaviours in the criterion setting, as informed by our understanding of the test construct. Depending on the construct, the test domain is typically defined in one of two ways. It can be defined operationally, as a set of practical, real-world tasks. Sampling then involves choosing the most characteristic tasks from the domain, for example, in terms of their frequency or importance. Alternatively, the domain can be defined in terms of a more abstract construct, for example, in terms of a theory of the components of knowledge and ability that underlie performance in the domain. For example, it may be defined in terms of knowledge of the grammatical system, or of vocabulary, or of features of pronunciation, or ability to perform aspects of the skill areas of speaking, listening, reading or writing. In this case, the test will sample, in a principled way, from a range of frequent grammatical structures or of items of vocabulary at the appropriate level, or will include each relevant skill area.

In the former case, if the performance domain is associated with particular known roles, for example, those occurring in a work or study skills setting, then a job analysis is carried out so that the communicative roles facing test-takers in the criterion situation can be determined and used as the basis for test design. This job analysis will typically involve eliciting the insights of those familiar with the target setting, for example, non-native speakers who are currently working within it. Other suitable informants will be job educators or trainers and other experts whose work requires them to have an articulated understanding of the character and demands of the setting. Methods used will include questionnaires and interview. It may also be possible to draw on a literature analysing the characteristics of the communicative demands of the setting; this is true in the area of medical communication, for example. When the job analysis has been completed, test materials will be written reflecting the domain, and a panel of experts who know the nature of the work involved may be asked to judge their relevance, coverage, and authenticity.

Test method

The next thing to consider in test design is the way in which candidates will be required to interact with the test materials, particularly the **response format**, that is, the way in which the candidate will be required to respond to the materials. (The term test method covers these aspects of design together with the issue of how candidate responses will be rated or scored.) There are two broad approaches to understanding the relation of test method to test content. The first sees method as an aspect of content, and raises issues of authenticity; the second, more traditional approach treats method independently of content, and allows more obviously inauthentic test response formats.

Authenticity of response

The job analysis discussed earlier will identify the range of communicative roles and tasks which characterize the criterion setting. This provides a basis not only for determining the kinds of texts to be included in the test, but also how candidates will interact with them. We may attempt to reproduce, as far as is possible in the test setting, the conditions under which they are processed or produced in reality. In this way, test method involves simulation of the criterion as much as other aspects of the test materials. The test method can itself become an aspect of relevant test content, if we define content not only in terms of the texts to be included but how they are used.

However, such an approach raises the issue of authenticity of response. There are competing imperatives. On the one hand it is desirable to replicate, as far as is possible in the test setting, the conditions under which engagement with communicative content is done in the criterion setting, so that inferences from the test performance to likely future performance in the criterion can be as direct as possible. On the other hand, it is necessary to have a procedure that is fair to all candidates, and elicits a scorable performance, even if this means involving the candidates in somewhat artificial behaviour. Once again, test design involves a sort of principled compromise. Let us consider this issue firstly in the context of assessing listening comprehension, and then in the context of the assessment of speaking.

In the development of a test of English as a foreign language for international students, a job analysis may reveal that listening to lectures is an important part of the candidates' future role as students, and so it makes sense to include listening to a lecture as part of the test. But how should evidence of such comprehension ability be sought? What form should the test task take? There are a number of possibilities:

1   The task replicates what students have to do in the target situation. The candidate is asked to take notes, which are then scored for the accuracy of their content. But students take notes in very different ways, some of which may cause difficulties in scoring. For example, if a particular person fails to make a note about a certain point, it may be because it has not been

understood, but it may also be because the note-taker has determined that it does not merit a note.

2 If candidates are required to answer pre-set questions, time might be given for reading them prior to the listening, or candidates might simply be required to read as they listen. If prior, either all the questions are presented at once, or a few are presented at a time. But if the latter, how many? That is, how long a chunk of lecture should the candidate have to process at any one time? Obviously, too long a stretch may introduce irrelevant memory considerations, and the test becomes as much a test of memory as of listening comprehension. On the other hand, if too short, then the task of following extended stretches of discourse is not represented in the test.

3 A candidate might be required to listen to the input just once, or more than once. Obviously repetition is unlike the real world in the sense that lectures are not repeated. On the other hand it may be argued that many students make a practice of audio-taping lectures to facilitate comprehension, recall, and note-taking following the lecture.

All decisions about test method in such a context inevitably involve a compromise between the desirability of an appearance of authenticity on the one hand and the practicalities imposed by the test situation on the other. Note that the way we resolve this compromise may have the undesired effect of jeopardizing the fairness of the conclusions we reach about individual candidates. For example, in the case where a candidate has been judged not to meet a required standard, might observation of his/her performance under more natural conditions have led us to a different conclusion? Methods of investigating the impact of decisions about test method on the fairness of our judgements will be taken up in Chapter 5 on validity.

In relation to the assessment of speaking, related questions of authenticity arise. Consider the case of immigrant non-native speaker teachers who will have to teach their subject area—science or mathematics, let us say—through the medium of a second language. Or consider teachers of foreign languages who wish to conduct their classes through the medium of the target language. In order to assess whether teachers in each group are communicatively competent to manage their classes in their second language, approaches ranging along a continuum of authenticity are conceivable.

Consider an aspect of classroom management, giving instructions for an activity. The most contrived, yet the most manageable from a test administration point of view, is to give a paper-and-pencil assessment of ability to handle this task, for example, by getting candidates to write out what they would say in giving such instructions. This might be an adequate test of candidates' control of the content of the instructions, but not give us any evidence about their ability to execute them, particularly in the context of interaction. Alternatively, we might attempt to simulate the task with a role-play simulation of giving instructions for the setting up of a specific classroom activity, perhaps in a one-to-one setting with an examiner playing the role of a student being given the instructions. More realistically still, we may require the teacher to teach an actual lesson, either with a specially assembled group of students, or in the context of an actual school lesson. Particular times and occasions of observation in the actual work setting may be agreed upon, for example during the course of school practice during a teacher training course. Alternatively, non-native speaker teachers in some cases may be given professional accreditation, and the adequacy of their proficiency in the second language to handle the communicative tasks of the work setting may be assessed over an extended period as part of an overall assessment of their readiness to practise their profession.

Obviously, as assessment becomes more authentic, it also becomes more expensive, complex, and potentially unwieldy. As assessment becomes more thoroughly contextualized, it is clear that a range of complex non-language-specific contextual variables will become relevant in such assessments, of the kind discussed in Chapter 2. This raises the difficult questions of validity discussed there, which will be considered further in Chapter 5.

Fixed and constructed response formats

An alternative to grappling with the dilemma of authenticity of response involves accepting to a greater or lesser degree the artificiality of the test situation, and using a range of conventional and possibly inauthentic test formats. Of course, this forces us to face the issue of the validity of the inferences we can make from performance within such formats.

Different response formats are sometimes conventionally associated with different types of test content. Tests of discrete points of grammar for example, often use multiple choice question (**MCQ**) format (see Chapter 1). MCQ is also commonly used in vocabulary tests; alternatively, lists of vocabulary items and possible definitions may be presented, with candidates having to match items and definitions. Usually there are unequal numbers of items and definitions, to prevent the last few matches becoming predictable through a process of elimination. Tests of reading and listening comprehension often use either one of the formats just discussed, or true-false formats, in which the candidates have to say whether a given proposition corresponds with one in the stimulus text or not. The propositions in the test question are based on rewordings of propositions in the text, not direct lifting of words or phrases from the text. Without paraphrase the task may require nothing more than a literal matching of similar words or phrases in the text and the question rather than an understanding of the meaning of the propositions involved.

In this section we have so far considered fixed response formats, that is, ones in which the candidates' possible responses have been anticipated and the candidate's task is to choose the appropriate response from those offered. **Constructed response formats** may also be used, although these are more complex and usually more expensive to score. For example, in a cloze test (see Chapter 2), candidates are required to fill in the blanks in the passage. In response to a stimulus comprehension passage, candidates may be asked to provide written or oral responses to **short answer questions**, in which they are responsible for the wording of the answer. Constructed response formats have the advantage of not constraining the candidate to the same degree, and reducing the effect of guessing. The candidate assumes greater responsibility for the response, and this may be perceived as in some ways more demanding and more authentic. The disadvantage of such response formats is that they are generally more expensive to score. They cannot be marked automatically by machine; and agreement among scorers on what constitutes an acceptable answer needs to be achieved. This may involve multiple marking of scripts and discussion of discrepancies. Even in scoring performances on a cloze test, decisions have to be made about the acceptability of responses other than the exact word originally deleted. Sometimes, another word may be equally acceptable in the gap; that is, it is syntactically and semantically appropriate. Determining the list of possible correct words and seeing that all scorers are applying the scoring procedure correctly is time consuming and therefore expensive. This takes us back to the issue of constraints mentioned above.

In the testing of productive skills, a further range of test method decisions need to be made, about the content and format of the stimulus to writing or speaking (the **prompt**), the length and format of the response, and about the scoring. For example, in writing assessment, decisions will need to be made about such matters as the number, length, and complexity of tasks set, the degree of support in terms of content provided, the source of ideas for content, where such support is provided, whether a choice of topic is permitted, and the exact wording of the instructions to candidates (the **rubric**). In addition, procedures for scoring, particularly the criteria against which the performance will be judged, need to be developed. If performances are to be judged against rating scales, then the scales need to be developed. What has been said here about writing also applies to the assessment of speaking skills, through interviews, role plays, group discussions, and other procedures. The assessment of productive skills is considered in detail in Chapter 4. Of course, much of what has been said in this paragraph applies as well to the design of relatively authentic tests of productive skills.

Test specifications

The result of the design process in terms of test content and test method is the creation of **test specifications**. These are a set of instructions for creating the test, written as if they are to be followed by someone other than the test developer; they are a recipe or blueprint for test construction. Their function is to force explicitness about the design decisions in the test and to allow new versions to be written in future. The specifications will include information on such matters as the length and structure of each part of the test, the type of materials with which candidates will have to engage, the source of such materials if authentic, the extent to which authentic materials may be altered, the response format, the test rubric, and how responses are to be scored. **Test materials** are then written according to the specifications, which may of course themselves be revised in the light of the writing process.

Test trials

The fourth stage is **trialling** or **trying out** the test materials and procedures prior to their use under operational conditions. This stage involves careful design of data collection to see how well the test is working. A trial population will have to be found, that is, a group of people who resemble in all relevant respects (age, learning background, general proficiency level, etc.) the target test population. With discrete point test items, a trial population of at least 100, and frequently far more than this, is required. Careful statistical analysis is carried out of responses to items to investigate their quality and the concepts. Some of the procedures involved are explained in Chapter 6. Where subjective judgements of speaking and writing are involved, there is a need for training of those making the judgements, and investigation of the interpretability and workability of the criteria and rating scales to be used. These issues are dealt with in detail in Chapter 4.

In addition, **test-taker feedback** should be gathered from the trial subjects, often by a simple questionnaire. This will include questions on perceptions of the level of difficulty of particular questions, the clarity of the rubrics, and general attitude to the materials and tasks. Subjects can quickly spot things that are problematic about materials which test developers struggle to see.

Materials and procedures will be revised in the light of the trials, in preparation for the operational use of the test. Data from actual test performances needs to be systematically gathered and analysed, to investigate the validity and usefulness of the test under operational conditions. Periodically, the results of this data gathering may lead to substantial revision of the test design, and the testing cycle will recommence. In any case, all new versions of the test need to be trialled, and monitored operationally. It is in the context of the testing cycle that most research on language testing is carried out.

Conclusion

In this chapter we have examined the process through which a testing procedure is conceptualized, developed, and put into operation. We have considered test content as an expression of test construct, and looked at how that content may be determined, especially through the procedures of job analysis. We have considered that the way in which candidates interact with test materials can also replicate real-world processes, and considered the issue of authenticity that arise. Often, in the interests of economy or manageability, particularly in large-scale tests, such replication is unaffordable, and more conventional response formats are the only option. We have considered a range of such formats here. In Chapter 4 we will consider in much greater detail the concepts and methods involved in judgements of performance in speaking and writing, and the issues of fairness that arise.

Throughout the testing cycle data for the investigation of test qualities are generated automatically in the form of responses to test items. The use of test data by researchers to question the fairness of the test takes us into the area of the validation of tests, which is the subject of Chapter 5.

4
The rating process

Making judgements about people is a common feature of every-day life. We are continually evaluating what others say and do, in comments called for or not, offering criticism and feedback informally to friends and colleagues about their behaviour. Formal, institutional judgements figure prominently in our lives too. People pass driving tests, survive the probationary period in a new job, get promotions at work, succeed at interviews, win Oscars for performances in a film, win medals in diving competitions, and are released from prison for good behaviour. The judgement will in most cases have direct consequences for the person judged, and so issues of fairness arise, which most public procedures try to take account of in some way. Regrettably, it is easy to become aware of the way in which the idiosyncrasies of the rater or the rating process can determine the outcome unfairly. In international sporting contests such as the Olympic Games and World Cup soccer, the nationality of judges, referees or umpires, and their presumed and sometimes real biases become an issue, and attempts are made to mitigate their effects. All of us can probably recount instances of the benign or damaging role of particular raters in examination processes in which we have been involved. Many people have anecdotes of bizarre procedures for reaching rating decisions in various contexts, for example in job selection.

This chapter will discuss rating procedures used in language assessment. (The terms **ratings** and raters will be used to refer to the judgements and those who make them.) We will discuss the necessity for, and pitfalls of, a rater-mediated approach to the assessment of language. First, we will look at the procedures used in judging, then at how judgements may be reported, and finally at threats to the fairness of the procedures and how these may be avoided or at least mitigated. We will consider in some detail three aspects of the validation of rating procedures: the establishment of rating protocols; exploring differences between individual raters, and mitigating their effects; and understanding interactions between raters and other features of the rating process (for example, the reactions of individual raters to particular topics or to speakers from a particular language background).

Establishing a rating procedure

Rater-mediated assessment is becoming more and more central to language teaching and learning. As communicative language teaching has increasingly focused on communicative performance in context, so rating the impact of that communication has become the focus of language assessment. Rater-mediated language assessment is also in line with institutional demands for accountability in education, as outcomes of educational processes are often described in terms of demonstrable practical competence in the learner. This competence is then verified through assessment.

Where assessments meet institutional requirements, for example for certification, as with any bureaucratic procedure there are set methods for yielding the judgement in question. These methods typically have three main aspects.

First, there is agreement about the conditions (including the length of time) under which the person's performance or behaviour is elicited, and/or is attended to by the rater. This may take the form of a formal examination, with set tasks and fixed amounts of time for the performances. Alternatively, it may involve a period of observation during instruction, or while candidates carry out relevant tasks and roles in the actual target performance context.

Second, certain features of the performance are agreed to be critical; the criteria for judging these will be determined and agreed. Usually this will involve considering various components of competence—*fluency, accuracy, organization, sociocultural appropriateness,* and so on. The weighting of each of the components of assessment becomes an issue. So does their relevance: an increasingly important question in the validation of performance assessments is how the relevant criteria for assessing the performance are to be decided. The heart of the test construct lies here.

Finally, raters who have been trained to an agreed understanding of the criteria characterize a performance by allocating a grade or rating. This assumes the prior development of descriptive rating categories of some kind: 'competent', 'not competent', 'ready to cope with a university course', and so on.

The problem with raters

Introducing the rater into the assessment process is both necessary and problematic. It is problematic because ratings are necessarily subjective. Another way of saying this is that the rating given to a candidate is a reflection, not only of the quality of the performance, but of the qualities as a rater of the person who has judged it. The assumption in most rating schemes is that if the rating category labels are clear and explicit, and the rater is trained carefully to interpret them in accordance with the intentions of the test designers, and concentrates while doing the rating, then the rating process can be made objective. In other words, rating is essentially reduced to a process of the recognition of objective signs, with classification following automatically. In this view rating would resemble the process of chicken sexing, in which young chicks are inspected for the external visible signs of their sex (apparent only to the trained eye when chicks are very young), and allocated to male and female categories accordingly.

But the reality is that rating remains intractably subjective. The allocation of individuals to categories is not a deterministic process, driven by the objective, recognizable characteristics of performances, external to the rater. Rather, rating always contains a significant degree of chance, associated with the rater and other factors. The influence of these factors can be explored by thinking of rating as a probabilistic phenomenon, that is, exploring the probabilities of certain rating outcomes with particular raters, particular tasks, and so on. We can easily show this by looking at the way in which even trained raters differ in their handling of the allocation of individual performances in borderline cases. Close comparison of the ratings given by different raters in such cases will typically show that one rater will be consistently inclined to assign a lower category to candidates whom another rater puts into a higher one. The obvious result of this is that whether a candidate is judged as meeting a particular standard or not depends fortuitously on which rater assesses their work. Worse (because this is less predictable), raters may not even be self-consistent from one assessed performance to the next, or from one rating occasion to another. Researchers have sometimes been dismayed to learn that there is as much variation among raters as there is variation between candidates.

In the 1950s and 1960s, when concerns for reliability dominated language assessment, rater-mediated assessment was discouraged because of the problem of subjectivity. This led to a tendency to avoid direct testing. Thus, writing skills were assessed indirectly through examination of control over the grammatical system and knowledge of vocabulary. But increasingly it was felt that so much was lost by this restriction on the scope of assessment that the problem of subjectivity was something that had to be faced and managed. Particularly with the advent of communicative language teaching, with its emphasis on how linguistic knowledge is actually put to use, understanding and managing the rating process became an urgent necessity.

Establishing a framework for making judgements

In establishing a rating procedure, we need to consider the criteria by which performances at a given level will be recognized, and then to decide how many different levels of performance we wish to distinguish. The answers to these questions will determine the basic framework or orientation for the rating process. Deciding which of these orientations best fits a particular assessment setting will depend on the context and purpose of the assessment.

It is useful to view achievement as a continuum. The assessment system may recognize a number of different levels of achievement, in which case we then think of it as representing a *ladder* or *scale*. In other contexts, only one point on the continuum is of relevance, and a simple 'enough/not enough' distinction is all that needs to be made. In this case the testing system can best be thought of in terms of a *hurdle* or **cut-point**. These two possibilities are not of course contradictory, but are a little like different settings on a camera or microscope. We can stand back and look at the whole continuum, or we can zoom in on one part of it. Each level of the ladder may be thought of as requiring a 'yes/no' decision ('enough/not enough') for that level.

We can illustrate the distinction between the hurdle and ladder perspectives by reference to two very different kinds of performance. Consider the driving test. Most people, given adequate preparation, would assume they could pass it. Although not everybody who passes the test has equal competence as a driver, the function of the test is to make a simple distinction between those who are safe on the roads and those who are not, rather than to distinguish degrees of competence in driving skill. Often, in hurdle assessments, as in the driving test, the assessment system is not intended to permanently exclude. In other words, every competent person should pass, and it is assumed that most people with adequate preparation will be capable of a competent performance, and derive the benefits of certification accordingly. The aim of the certification is to protect other people from incompetence. The assessment is essentially not competitive.

Many systems of assessment try to combine the characteristics of access and competition. For example, in the system of certification for competence in piano playing, a number of grades of performance are established, with relevant criteria defining each, and over a number of years a learner of the piano may proceed through the examinations for the grades. As the levels become more demanding, fewer people have the necessary motivation or opportunity to prepare for performance at such a level, or indeed even the necessary skill. The final stages of certification involve fiercely contested piano competitions where only the most brilliant will succeed, so resembling the Olympic context. But at levels below this, the 'grade' system of certification involves a principle of access: at each step of competence, judged in a 'yes'/'no' manner ('competent at this level' vs. 'not competent'), those with adequate preparation are likely to pass. The function of the assessment at a given level is not to make distinctions between candidates, other than a binary distinction between those who meet the requirements of the level and those who do not.

Language testing has examples of each of these kinds of framework for making judgements about individuals. In judgements of competence, to perform particular kinds of occupational roles, for example to work as a medical practitioner through the medium of a second language, where the communicative demands of the work or study setting to which access is sought are high, then the form of the judgement will be 'ready' or 'not ready', as in the driving test. Even though the amount of preparation is much greater, and what is demanded is much higher, we nevertheless expect each of the medical professionals who present for such a test to succeed in the end. Its function is not usually to exclude permanently those who need to demonstrate competence in the language in order to practise their profession, although tests may of course be used as instruments of such exclusion, as we shall see later, in Chapter 7. In contrast, in contexts where only a small percentage of candidates can be selected, for example in the awarding of competitive prizes or scholarships, then the higher levels of achievement will become important as they are used to distinguish the most able of candidates from the rest. This is the case in contexts of achievement, for example, in school-based language learning, or in vocational and workplace training.

Rating scales

Most often, frameworks for rating are designed as scales, as this allows the greatest flexibility to the users, who may want to use the multiple distinctions available from a scale, or who may choose to focus on only one cut-point or region of the scale. The preparation of such a scale involves developing **level descriptors**, that is, describing in words performances that illustrate each level of competence defined on the scale. For example, in the driving test, performance at a passing level might be described as 'Can drive in normal traffic conditions for 20 minutes making a range of normal movements and dealing with a range of typical eventualities; and can cope with a limited number of frequently encountered suddenly emerging situations on the road.' This description will necessarily be abstracted from the experience of those familiar with the setting and its demands, in this case experienced driving instructors, and will have to be vetted by a relevant authority entrusted with (in this case) issuing a licence to drive based on the test performance.

An ordered series of such descriptions is known as a **rating**

scale. A number of distinctions are usually made—rating scales typically have between 3 and 9 levels. Figure 4.1 gives an example of a summary rating scale developed by the author to describe levels of performance on an advanced level test of English as a second language for speaking skills in clinical settings.

Aspect of performance considered: overall communicative effectiveness

---

1 elementary level of communicative effectiveness

2 clearly could not cope in a bridging programme in a clinical setting involving interactions with patients and colleagues

3 just below minimum competence needed to cope in a bridging programme in a clinical setting involving interactions with patients and colleagues

4 has minimum competence needed to cope in a bridging programme in a clinical setting involving interactions with patients and colleagues

5 could easily cope in a bridging programme in a clinical setting involving interactions with patients and colleagues

6 near native communicative effectiveness

FIGURE 4.1 *Rating scale, Occupational English Test for health professionals*

This rating scale is used as part of a screening procedure (used to determine if an overseas trained health professional has the necessary minimum language skills to be admitted under supervision to the clinical setting). In this particular case, as the focus of the discriminations made in the scale is around a single point of minimum competence, the other levels tend to be defined in terms of their distance from this point. Most rating scales do not have such a single point of reference, and ideally the definition of each level should be independent of the ones above and below it on the scale. In fact, however, given the continuous nature of the scale, wordings frequently involve comparative statements, with one level described relative to one or more others—for example, in terms of greater or less control of features of the grammatical system, or pronunciation, and so on.

An important aspect of a scale is the way in which performance at the top end of the scale is defined. There is frequently an unacknowledged problem here. Rating scales often make reference to what are assumed to be the typical performances of native speakers or expert users of the language at the top end of the scale. That is, it is assumed that the performance of native speakers will be fundamentally unlike the performances of non-native speakers, who will tend gradually to approximate native speaker performance as their own proficiency increases. However, claims about the uniformly superior performance of these idealized native speakers have rarely been supported empirically. In fact, the studies that have been carried out typically show the performance of native speakers as highly variable, related to educational level, and covering a range of positions on the scale. In spite of this, the idealized view of native speaker performance still hovers inappropriately at the top of many rating scales.

The number of levels on a rating scale is also an important matter to consider, although the questions raised here are more a matter of practical utility than of theoretical validity. There is no point in proliferating descriptions outside the range of ability of interest. Having too few distinctions within the range of such ability is also frustrating, and the revision of rating scales often involves the creation of more distinctions.

The failure of rating scales to make distinctions sufficiently fine to capture progress being made by students is a frequent problem. It arises because the purposes of users of a single assessment instrument may be at odds. Teachers have continuous exposure to their students' achievements in the normal course of learning. In the process, they receive ongoing informal confirmation of learner progress which may not be adequately reflected in a category difference as described by a scale. Imagine handing parents who are seeking evidence of their child's growth a measuring stick with marks on it only a foot (30 centimetres) apart, the measure not allowing any other distinction to be made. The parents can observe the growth of the child: they have independent evidence in the comments of relatives, or the fact that the child has grown out of a set of clothes. Yet in terms of the measuring stick no growth can be recorded because the child has not passed the magic cut-point into the next adjacent category of measurement.

Teachers restricted to reporting achievement only in terms of broad rating scale categories are in a similar position. Most rating scales used in public educational settings are imposed by government authorities for purposes of administrative efficiency and financial accountability, for which fine-grained distinctions are unnecessary. The scales are used to report the achievements of the educational system in terms of changes in the proficiency of large numbers of learners over relatively extended periods of time. The government needs the 'big picture' of learner (and teacher) achievement in order to satisfy itself that its educational budget is yielding results. Teachers working with these government-imposed, scale-based reporting mechanisms experience frustrations with the lack of fine distinctions on the scale. The coarse-grained character of the categories may hardly do justice to the teachers' sense of the growth and learning that has been achieved in a course. The purposes of the two groups—administrators, who are interested in financial accountability, and teachers, who are interested in the learning process may be at odds in such a case.

The wording of rating scales may vary according to the purposes for which they are to be used. On the one hand, scales are used to guide and constrain the behaviour of raters, and on the other, they are used to report the outcome of a rating process to score users—teachers, employers, admission authorities, parents, and so on. As a result different versions of a rating scale are often created for different users.

Holistic and analytic ratings

Performances are complex. Judgement of performances involves balancing perceptions of a number of different features of the performance. In speaking, a person may be fluent, but hard to understand; another may be correct, but stilted. Thus rather than getting raters to record a single impression of the impact of the performance as a whole (**holistic rating**), an alternative approach involves getting raters to provide separate assessments for each of a number of aspects of performance. For example, in speaking, raters may be asked to provide separate assessments of: fluency, appropriateness, pronunciation, control of formal resources of grammar, and vocabulary and the like. This latter approach is known as **analytic rating**, and requires the development of a number of separate rating scales for each aspect assessed. Even where analytic rating is carried out, it is usual to combine the scores for the separate aspects into a single overall score for reporting purposes. This single reporting scale may maintain its analytic orientation in that the overall characterization of a level description may consist of a weaving together of strands relating to separate aspects of performance.

Rater training

An important way to improve the quality of rater-mediated assessment schemes is to provide initial and ongoing training to raters. This usually takes the form of a **moderation** meeting. At such a meeting, individual raters are each initially asked to provide independent ratings for a series of performances at different levels. They are then confronted with the differences between the ratings they have given and those given by the other raters in the group. Discrepancies are noted and are discussed in detail, with particular attention being paid to the way in which the level descriptors are being interpreted by individual raters. Moderation meetings have the function of bringing about broad agreement on the relevant interpretation of level descriptors and rating categories.

Even where agreement is reached on the meaning of terms, there remain differences between raters. This may be in terms of relative severity, or a consistent tendency to see a particular performance as narrowly demonstrating or narrowly failing to demonstrate achievement at a particular performance level. The more extreme cases of rater harshness or leniency will emerge in rater training. Usually, the psychological pressure of embarrassment over having given ratings out of line with those of others is sufficient to get raters to reduce their differences. After an initial moderation meeting raters are typically given a further set of training performances to rate, and are accredited as raters if these ratings show adequate conformity with agreed ratings for the performances in question. Ongoing monitoring of rater performance is clearly necessary to ensure fairness in the testing process.

Conclusion

In this chapter we have accepted the desirability of rater-mediated assessment, and looked at issues in the design of rating procedures. We have looked at the construction and use of rating scales to guide rater behaviour, and noted the enormous potential for variability and hence unfairness in the rating process, associated for example with task and rater factors. Rater-mediated assessment is complex and in a way ambitious in its goals, and requires a sophisticated understanding of the ways in which it can be unfair to candidates and ways unfairness can be avoided.

5

Validity: testing the test

As we have seen, testing is a matter of using data to establish evidence of learning. But evidence does not occur concretely in the natural state, so to speak, but is an abstract inference. It is a matter of judgement. The question arises as to who makes this judgement, and how we can decide how valid the evidence is. The very terms judgement and evidence suggest a court of law, and one way of making the issues clear is to draw parallels between testing and legal procedures.

In the famous American murder trial of the athlete O.J. Simpson, the jury was asked to determine, on the basis of the evidence presented, whether the police and prosecutor's claim that he had been involved in the murder of his wife and her friend was likely to be true ('beyond reasonable doubt'). The death of his wife and her friend had been witnessed by no-one apart from the victims themselves and the killer, so that reconstruction of what actually happened had to be done by inference. This was initially done by the police investigating the case, who came to the conclusion, on the evidence available to them, that the likely killer was O.J. Simpson. He was thus charged with murder. In the trial, the police procedures and the conclusions they had reached on the basis of the evidence were themselves put to the test. In the event, the jury decided there was enough doubt to acquit Simpson. In criminal procedures such as this, there are thus two stages, each involving the consideration of evidence. First, the police make an investigation, and on the evidence available to them reach the conclusion that a crime has been committed by someone, who is then charged. This conclusion is itself then examined, using an independent procedure (often a trial with a jury).

These two stages are mirrored in language test development and validation. The initial stage is represented by the test itself, in which the evidence of test performance is used to reach a conclusion about the candidate's ability to handle the demands of the criterion situation. (Remember, as we saw in Chapter 1, we are never in a position to observe those subsequent performances directly.) In some tests, matters are sometimes left there; the test procedures are not themselves subject to scrutiny, that is, they are not validated. Where a lot hinges on the determinations made in a language test, for example, where it is used to screen for admission to academic or work settings (such tests are sometimes called **high stakes tests**), measures may similarly be taken to investigate the procedures by which test judgements were reached. This process is known as test validation.

The purpose of validation in language testing is to ensure the defensibility and fairness of interpretations based on test performance. It asks, 'On what basis is it proposed that individuals be admitted or denied access to the criterion setting being sought? Is this a sufficient or fair basis?' In the case of both legal and assessment settings, the focus of investigation is on the procedures used. If the procedures are faulty, then conclusions about particular individuals are likely to be unsound. The scrutiny of such procedures will involve both reasoning and examination of the facts. In the legal case, the reasoning may involve legal argumentation, and appeals to the common sense, insight, and human understanding of the jury members, as well as careful examination of the evidence. Test validation similarly involves thinking about the logic of the test, particularly its design and its intentions, and also involves looking at empirical evidence—the hard facts—emerging from data from test trials or operational administrations. If no validation procedures are available there is potential for unfairness and injustice. This potential is significant in proportion to what is at stake.

There are certain differences between the two contexts. First, legal cases usually involve an individual accused; test validation looks at the procedures as a whole, for all the candidates affected by them. Secondly, in the case of a crime, the picture being formed in the minds of the police concerns something that has already happened, that is, it is retrospective. This is replicated only in certain kinds of tests, but not in others. We saw in Chapter 1 that we can distinguish tests according to their purpose, and defined one such type of test, an achievement test, as retrospective, giving evidence on what has been achieved. The inferences from proficiency tests on the other hand are predictive or forward looking, as such tests typically precede entry to the criterion setting, as in selection, screening, and certification tests. As we saw in Chapter 1, inferences are made from these tests about how a person is likely to manage the language and communicative demands of the subsequent non-test or criterion situation, for example, listening to lectures (in the role of international student), or communicating with colleagues or clients (in work-related language assessments).

There is also a contrast in the allocation of roles to individuals in the two settings. In the legal setting, the arguments for and against the charge are presented by different individuals, the prosecution and defence lawyers. The persons making the decision (the jury or the judge) are independent of either. The person who has most at stake—the accused—is directly represented. In the test situation, the prosecution, defence, judge, and jury are all the same person—the person responsible for the validation research; moreover, this is often the test developer, who may be seen as having a vested interest in the test surviving the challenge of validation. Of course, validation research may be presented to a wider audience of other researchers in the form of conference papers or publications in academic journals, in which case it may encounter further challenges; this is the function of the discourse community of language testing researchers. As test validation involves close analysis of test data, it is necessarily technical, and its function too easily misunderstood or discounted, particularly by those funding the test, who may wish to do without the complication and expense of carrying it out. Many public tests with a significant burden of responsibility in important decision making about individuals have been too little validated as a result.

The research carried out to validate test procedures can accompany test development, and is often done by the test developers themselves; that is, it can begin before the test becomes operational. Validation ideally continues through the life of the test, as new questions about its validity arise, usually in the context of language testing research.

In some public discussions of new test procedures, particularly those fulfilling a role in public policy, the term validation is sometimes used rather differently. It refers to the process of negotiating the acceptability of a new assessment procedure to the **stakeholders**, that is, those most interested in its introduction. For example, if a new testing procedure is being introduced as a matter of government policy, then it may be politically important to ensure its acceptability to educators and administrators. In this case, the scales and frameworks used in such procedures, or even actual sample test materials, may be distributed in draft and become the subject of intense discussion of their content and wording. This process may result in valuable revisions to the materials, but its deeper function is to ensure that nobody is too unhappy with the change; the 'validation' is designed to defuse opposition. This procedure guarantees the **face validity** of the test (its surface acceptability to those involved in its development or use) but no more.

Threats to test validity

Why are test validation procedures necessary? Why is face validity not enough? What can threaten the validity—the meaningfulness, interpretability, and fairness of assessments (scores, ratings)? Let us look at a number of possible problem areas, to do with test *content* (what the test contains; see Chapter 3), test *method* (the way in which the candidate is asked to engage with the materials and tasks in the test, and how these responses will be scored; see also Chapter 3), and test *construct* (the underlying ability being captured by the test; see Chapter 2).

Test content

The issue here is the extent to which the test content forms a satisfactory basis for the inferences to made from test performance. We saw in Chapter 3 how content relevance can be established in well designed tests. These procedures are used to establish the relevance of what candidates are asked to do. Imagine that you are working as a flight attendant for an international airline. On certain routes passengers may need assistance in their own language in the course of the flight. The airline has thus decided to give bonuses to flight attendants who can demonstrate a given level of proficiency in the languages most frequently spoken by passengers on that airline. As such assistance rarely involves reading and writing, and is on the whole restricted to a range of predictable topics, it would be unreasonable to test potential employees on communication tasks not found in that setting, or on tasks presented through an inappropriate mode of language use (reading, writing). On the one hand, even if a potential employee could manage such test tasks, it may not be safe to infer that the person concerned can communicate adequately on non-tested oral tasks more relevant to the occupational role. And vice versa: if the person fails the test tasks, he/she may still be fluent orally—this would be so in the case of languages with different alphabets or writing systems, particularly where the person's acquisition of the language has been through informal means.

The issues arising in such contexts are issues of what is known as content-related validity or, more traditionally, **content validity**. The argument for the relevance of test content to the decisions to be made about functioning in the criterion situation has led to the growth of specific purpose language tests, such as the Occupational English Test for health professionals wishing to work in Australia.

Judgements as to the relevance of content are often quite complex, and the validation effort is accordingly elaborate. For example, in a test of ability to read academic texts, does it matter from which academic domain the texts are drawn? Should someone studying law be asked to read texts drawn from fields such as education or medicine? In other contexts, we may want to know whether performance on a general proficiency test can be used to predict performance in particular occupational roles, and vice versa. Sometimes, there is pressure from bureaucracies to use tests designed for one purpose to make decisions in a very different context that had not been envisioned by the original test designers. The problem is that the inferences we draw about candidates based on a test designed for one purpose are not necessarily valid for another unrelated purpose, particularly where test content reflects the original test purpose.

Test method and test construct

How are the test-takers required to engage with the test materials? To what extent are arbitrary features of the test method influencing the inferences we are reaching about candidates? We saw in Chapter 2 the kinds of choices about test method open to test designers. We also saw that the most commonly used methods involve considerable compromise on the authenticity of the test, so that the gap between test performance and performance in the criterion may, on the face of it, appear quite wide. What implications does our choice of test method have on the inferences we make about candidates?

One way of approaching this issue is to ask to what extent the method is properly part of the test construct (the underlying ability or trait being measured by the test), or is irrelevant to it. If the latter is the case (and it often necessarily is), then we need to investigate the impact of test method on scores, because if the impact is large, then it has the potential to obscure our picture of the relevant aspects of candidate abilities. This will involve a programme of research, for example, by varying the conditions of performance. Thus, in the case of the note-taking task, we can compare scores obtained from comparable groups of subjects under various conditions of interest and study the resulting impact on scores. We can see whether scores are affected when candidates are allowed unconstrained vs. constrained note-taking, are exposed to shorter versus longer chunks of text at any one time, are required to pre-read the questions or not, listen once or more than once to the test materials, and so on.

In the case of speaking and writing, even when test content and methods used to elicit a performance seem reasonable, other aspects of the testing procedure can jeopardize the meaningfulness of test inferences. We saw in Chapter 4, for example, that rating procedures introduce a host of variables into the assessment. Research on rating is part of the validation required for performance tests of this type. In general, the more complex the context of performance, the more there is to jeopardize the validity of the ratings. This point was well recognized by Lado in the 1950s and 1960s (see Chapter 2), and is what made him so wary of performance assessment.

In general, tests may introduce factors that are irrelevant to the aspect of ability being measured (**construct irrelevant variance**); or they may require too little of the candidate (**construct under-representation**). There may be factors in the test which will cause performances to be affected, or to vary in a way which is not relevant to the information being sought about candidates' abilities. Thus, as we have seen, the knowledge or skill being tested may be embedded in a context which is neither within the candidate's experience nor relevant to the thing being assessed. In an advanced level oral test, candidates may be asked to speak on an abstract topic; however, if the topic does not match their interests or is one about which they may have little knowledge, the performance is likely to appear less impressive than when candidates are speaking about a more familiar topic at an equivalent level of abstraction. In this case, then, a potential problem is that the trait being assessed (ability to discuss an abstract topic in the foreign language) is confounded with the irrelevant requirement of having knowledge of a particular topic.

By contrast, in other cases, the real requirements of the criterion may not be fully represented in the test. Take the case of foreign medical graduates in the UK or Australia, who face practical clinical examinations where they must take case histories from real patients. Examiners frequently complain that the candidates' communicative skills are not up to the task, even though they will have passed a prior test, and, on this measure, seem to have a high degree of language ability. Clearly, something which the clinicians feel is important in communication with patients is missing from the language test.

The impact of tests

In the last decade, a renewed theory of test validation has expanded the scope of validation research to include the changes that may occur as a consequence of their introduction. Such changes (for example in preparation of test candidates) may in turn have an impact on what is being measured by the test, in such a way that the fairness of inferences about candidates is called into question. This area is known as the **consequential validity** of tests. For example, in a school context, an assessment reform which changes the emphasis from formal tests to ongoing assessment of complex projects and assignments may raise issues of consequential validity if it turns out that students can be coached into performance on the projects, and the opportunities for coaching are differentially available to the students being assessed (for example, because only some families can afford coaching, or because children with more highly educated parents get help from their parents). What appears initially to be a test reform may thus in the end have the unfortunate and obviously unintended effect of reducing our ability to make meaningful distinctions between students in terms of the abilities being measured. To the extent that such consequences can be foreseen, the test developer is bound to anticipate them and investigate their likely effect on the validity of test scores. Concerns about consequential validity are part of a larger area of research on the impact of assessment procedures on teaching and learning, and more broadly on society as a whole. The social context of assessment will be considered in detail in Chapter 7.

Conclusion

In this chapter we have examined the need for questioning the bases for inferences about candidate abilities residing in test procedures, and the way in which these inferences may be at risk from aspects of test design and test method, or lack of clarity in our thinking about what we are measuring. Efforts to establish the validity of tests has generated much of what constitutes the field of language testing research. Such research involves two primary techniques: speculation and empiricism. Speculation here refers to reasoning and logical analysis about the nature of language and language use, and of the nature of performance, of the type that we outlined in Chapter 2. Empiricism means subjecting such theorizing and specific implications of particular testing practices to examination in the light of data from test trials and operational test administrations. Thus, as an outcome of the test development cycle, language testing research involves the formation of hypotheses about the nature of language ability, and putting such hypotheses to the test. In this way, language testing is rescued from being a merely technical activity and constitutes a site for research activity of a fundamental nature in applied linguistics.

6
Measurement

Introduction

Assessment usually involves allocating a score, an attractively simple number. Gertrude Stein tells us that 'A rose is a rose is a rose', but measurement people (in their unimaginative way) tell us that a score is not a score is not a score: scores can be deceptive. For example, when different raters give the same score, do they mean the same thing? In tests with several parts and multiple items, how consistent are score patterns across different parts of a test? Can we add scores from the different parts, or across tests of different sub-skills, or are they measuring such different things that they are incommensurable, cannot be talked about in the same breath? What do the scores on a test tell us about its quality, and its suitability for its intended purpose? These are questions addressed by measurement, the theoretical and empirical analysis of scores and score meaning.

Often, when people think (if they do) about testing, they perceive it as a dauntingly technical field, and it is often the measurement aspect of the field that puts people off. 'Means', 'percentiles', 'standard deviations', statistics—these inspire a lack of confidence that one could ever (or indeed would ever want to) engage successfully with testing as an area of knowledge and expertise. Yet, curiously, concepts from the field of measurement can be found frequently in everyday conversation: 'She is of above average intelligence.' 'He topped his class.' 'It's like saying that these apples are not very good oranges.' 'He's a not a reliable judge.' It is not so much then, that people are not interested in the questions that measurement asks, as that they are daunted by the way it goes about answering them, by its procedures and language. The aim of this chapter is to give a brief introduction to a small selection of measurement concepts and procedures commonly used in language assessment, and in particular to make the reader feel that they are accessible and worth understanding.

Measurement

Measurement investigates the quality of the process of assessment by looking at scores. Two main steps are involved:

1 Quantification, that is, the assigning of numbers or scores to various outcomes of assessment. The set of scores available for analysis when data are gathered from a number of test-takers is known as a **data matrix**.

2 Checking for various kinds of mathematical and statistical patterning within the matrix in order to investigate the extent to which necessary properties (for example, consistency of performance by candidates, or by judges) are present in the assessment.

The aim of these procedures is to achieve quality control, that is, to improve the meaningfulness and fairness of the conclusions reached about individual candidates (the validity of the test). Measurement procedures have no rationale other than to underpin validity.

Quality control for raters

As an example of what measurement expertise can contribute to our understanding of language tests, and our ability to develop fair and meaningful tests, we will look at the question of quality control procedures for raters. To what extent is there agreement between raters, and where there is disagreement, what can be done about it?

As investigation of rater agreement depends on the comparison of ratings, the first step involves careful data collection. A rating design is prepared in which raters are asked to carry out a number of ratings, with overlap between raters so that they each independently rate the same performances. In this way the ratings of one rater can be compared with the ratings of others.

Imagine a rating system (suggestive of the fiction of Franz Kafka) in which the ratings which candidates get depend not at all on the quality of their performances, but entirely on the whim of the rater. Occasionally, the rating would (by chance) be fair, but mostly it would not, and one would never know which rating accidentally reflected the candidate's ability, and which did not. The ratings would be entirely unreliable. Looked at mathematically, the ratings of one rater for a set of performances would bear little relationship to those of another, and would not be predictable from them. The reason for this is that the only thing causing differences in scores is the whim of individual raters, not the quality of the performance, to which the rater is indifferent.

Imagine the opposite (and equally fanciful) case of the ideal rating system. In this case, the only thing driving the ratings is the quality of the performance, so it shouldn't matter who the judge is, as he/she will recognize that quality and allocate the performance to the appropriate rating category accordingly. Looked at mathematically, in such a situation the ratings of any individual rater for a set of performances would be perfectly predictable from knowledge of the ratings given to those performances by another rater; they would be identical. If I wanted to know how candidate Laura fared with Rater B, I need only find out how she fared with Rater A and I would know.

In reality, the situation will lie somewhere between these two extremes. But exactly where? How much dependable information on the quality of performances do scores from a rater contain, and how much do they reflect the whim of that rater? Measurement methods can help us tackle this question very precisely. They can do so because they can draw on mathematical methods for exploring the extent to which one set of measures is predictable from another set for the same class of individuals or objects.

Such mathematical methods for establishing predictable numerical relations of this kind originated in the rather prosaic field of agriculture, in order to explore the predictive relationship between varying amounts of fertilizer and associated crop yields. But the methods apply equally well to human beings, for example, in working out the extent to which the weight of a set of adult males of a given age group is predictable from their height. A set of **statistics** or single summary figures has been developed to capture any such predictive relationship. One of these, the **correlation coefficient** r, is frequently used in language assessment. It expresses the extent to which one score set is knowable from another, and uses a scale from o (no correspondence between the score sets at all, as in the Kafkaesque situation) to 1 (perfect correspondence, as in the ideal rating system). When used to express the extent of predictability of ratings between raters, and hence inter-rater agreement, this coefficient is called a **reliability coefficient** and expresses **inter-rater reliability**. Let us say we calculate this coefficient for each pairing of raters who are taking part in the rating scheme, and come up with some figures on the o to 1 scale. How are we to interpret these figures? And what level of reliability as expressed by the statistic should we be demanding of these raters?

Benchmarks for minimum acceptable inter-rater agreement range from 0.7 to 0.9 on this scale, depending on what is at stake, and what other information about candidates we may have (for example, their scores on other parts of the test). 0.7 represents a rock-bottom minimum of acceptable agreement between raters: this value can be understood as representing about 50% agreement and 50% disagreement between a pair of raters—hardly impressive. 0.9 is a much more satisfactory level (representing about 80% agreement, 20% disagreement overall); but achieving this level among raters may involve careful attention to the clear wording of criteria and rigorous training of raters in their interpretation.

Obviously, it is useful to have a commonly understood scale for expressing the degree of rater agreement in this way. It allows for ready communication about the extent to which one can depend on ratings from any assessment scheme involving raters, and to set standards. It also allows you to study the impact of rater training in improving rater reliability, to identify individual raters whose ratings are inconsistent with those of others, to provide certification for consistent raters, and to have confidence, once overall levels of agreement are high, in the workability of the rating scheme.

Correlation coefficients are not the only means of studying agreement between raters. When a single classification decision is to be made, a **classification analysis** can be carried out. This is a very simple procedure which can easily be done by hand. Imagine two raters (A and B) each of whom independently rates a set of performances from 30 candidates. They are required to say whether the performance demonstrates a required level of competence, or otherwise. A table is drawn up, setting out the rating categories ('Competent'/'Not Competent') available to each rater, and the frequency of agreement and disagreement between the raters, as in Figure 6.1

Rater A

		Competent	Not competent
Rater B	Competent	||||||||||||| [= 13]	||| [= 3]
	Not competent	|||| [= 4]	|||||||||| [= 10]

FIGURE 6.1 *Classification analysis for two raters*

The pairs of ratings for each candidate's performance are considered in turn. Where there is agreement that the performance demonstrates competence, a mark is made in the upper left hand cell in the table; where the raters agree that the performance fails to demonstrate competence, a mark is made in the lower right cell. The cases of disagreement are similarly noted. The number of marks in each cell is then totalled. In this case, the raters agreed about 23 of the 30 performances, and disagreed about 7. We can then report this as percentage agreement: 23/30 = 77%.

Where more than two classification categories are available, the above kind of information on frequency of misclassification can be complemented by information on how far apart the raters were in particular instances—one level apart, two levels apart, and so on. This information can be used in rater training, rater certification, and research, as with the inter-rater reliability coefficients discussed above.

There are a range of further and more complex statistical analyses procedures for the investigation of ratings which we need not go into here: they can be taken as more elaborate variations on the same basic themes.

Investigating the properties of individual test items

While investigating rater characteristics is important in guaranteeing the meaningfulness and fairness of assessment in performance tests, other kinds of quality control procedures are necessary in paper-and-pencil tests (for this distinction, see Chapter 1; for item formats, see Chapter 4). In tests with a number of individual objectively scored test items, for example, in tests of language comprehension, or tests of knowledge of individual points of grammar or vocabulary, it is usual to carry out a procedure known as **item analysis**. This procedure involves the careful analysis of score patterns on each of the test items. The analysis tells us how well each item is working, that is, the contribution it is making to the overall picture of candidates' ability emerging from the test.

Item analysis is a normal part of test development. Before a test is introduced in its final format, a **pilot version** of the test is developed. This will contain a number of draft items (many more than are needed, so that only the best ones will survive the piloting), possibly in a variety of item formats of interest. This version is then taken by a group of individuals with the same learner profile as the ultimate test-takers (the number has to be sufficiently large for analyses of patterns of responses to items to be possible). This stage of test development is known as a trialling or trying out. The effectiveness of items (and hence of formats) is evaluated using the item analysis procedures described later in this chapter, and the test revised before the **operational version** of the test (the version that will actually be used in test administrations with candidates) is finalized.

Item analysis usually provides two kinds of information on items:

> **item facility**, which helps us decide if test items are at the right level for the target group, and
>
> **item discrimination**, which allows us to see if individual items are providing information on candidates' abilities consistent with that provided by the other items on the test.

Item facility expresses the proportion of the people taking the test who got a given item right. (**Item difficulty** is sometimes used to express similar information, in this case the proportion who got an item wrong.) Where the test purpose is to make distinctions between candidates, to spread them out in terms of their performance on the test, the items should be neither too easy nor too difficult. If the items are too easy, then people with differing levels of ability or knowledge will all get them right, and the differences in ability or knowledge will not be revealed by the item. Similarly, if the items are too hard, then able and less able candidates alike will get them wrong, and the item won't help us in distinguishing between them. Item facility is expressed on a scale from 0 (no-one got the item right) to 1 (everybody got it right); for example, an item facility of 0.37 means that 37% of those who took the item got it right. Ideal item facility is 0.5 but of course it is hard to hit this target exactly, and a range of item facilities from 0.33 to 0.66 is usually accepted. Even though, as we have seen, items that are very easy (items with high item facility) don't distinguish between candidates, it may be useful to include some at the beginning of a test in order to ease candidates into the test and to allow them a chance to get over their nerves. It may also be worth including a few rather hard items near the end of the test in order to distinguish between the most able candidates, if that information is relevant, for example in deciding who shall get prizes in a competitive examination.

Analysis of **item discrimination** addresses a different target: consistency of performance by candidates across items. The usual method for calculating item discrimination involves comparing performance on each item by different groups of test-takers: those who have done well on the test overall, and those who have done relatively poorly. For example, as items get harder, we would expect those who do best on the test overall to be the ones who in the main get them right. Poor item discrimination indices are a signal that an item deserves revision.

If there are a lot of items with problems of discrimination, the information coming out of the test is confusing, as it means that some items are suggesting certain candidates are relatively better, while others are indicating that other individuals are better; no clear picture of the candidates' abilities emerges from the test. (The scores, in other words, are misleading, and not reliable indicators of the underlying abilities of the candidates.) Such a test will need considerable revision. The overall capacity of a multi-item test such as a comprehension test or a test of grammar or vocabulary to define levels of knowledge or ability among candidates consistently is referred to as the **reliability** of the test. As with the rater-mediated assessment indices discussed above, a statistical index known as a **reliability coefficient** is available to express on a scale of 0 to 1 the extent to which the test overall is succeeding in these terms. This index is broadly interpretable in the same way as the inter-rater reliability indices discussed above. We normally look for reliabilities on comprehension tests, or on tests of grammar or vocabulary, of 0.9 or better. A reliability of 0.9 means that scores on the test are providing about 80% reliable information on candidates' abilities, with about 20% attributable to randomness or error.

Norm-referenced and criterion-referenced measurement

Approaches to testing can be defined in terms of the broad measurement assumptions they make. Two approaches are particularly relevant within language testing: **norm-referenced** and **criterion-referenced measurement**.

Norm-referenced measurement adopts a framework of comparison between individuals for understanding the significance of any single score. Each score is seen in the light of other scores, particularly in terms of its frequency (how often such a score typically occurs in a much larger group of test-takers). In daily life we operate with an idea of typical frequencies of occurrence for particular values of height, weight, and so on. For example, you will hear people saying 'That little girl is tall for her age' or 'He's rather overweight' or 'She's average looking.' We have internalized a sense of how often we will see young men of a range of heights. Men of average height are so common as to be unremarkable; exceptionally tall men—for example, athletes in sports where height may be an advantage are often the subject of comment. The typical distribution of height in this population of young men is well recognized, for example, by shopkeepers selling men's clothing, who will keep abundant stock of trousers with the most common leg measurements, but far fewer items of unusual size which would fit basketball champions or jockeys.

If we carefully measured the height of a large number of subjects from the population of interest, we could keep count of how frequently measurement within given ranges of height occurred. In other words, we could develop information on the distribution of these frequencies of occurrences of heights across the men we had measured. Statisticians interested in measurement have done just this for a number of biological attributes, and it turns out that the distribution in each case is broadly similar. Statisticians have attempted to capture these typical frequencies in an idealized format known as the **normal distribution**. The highest frequencies occur near the average (or mean), and known proportions occur at given distances either side of the mean, thus giving the curve of the distribution its well-known bell shape (cf. Figure 6.2). The mathematical character of the normal distribution has been intensively studied for decades, and has predictable properties which can then be applied in measurement.

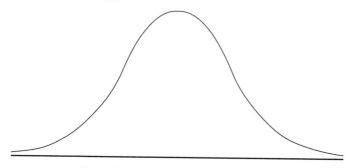

FIGURE 6.2 *The bell curve of the normal distribution*

Norm-referenced approaches to measurement assume that test scores will be like height or other biological measures, that is, normally distributed across the population of interest. Most scores will be around the average, and the further away from the average a score is, the more unusual it is likely to be. Thus, in norm-referenced measurement, an individual performance is evaluated not in terms of its quality compared with some criterion performance ('Did it meet what was required?') but in terms of its typicality for the population in question ('How good was it compared with the performances of others?').

Norm-referenced measurement has several advantages. In contexts where this is appropriate it allows for distinct levels of performance to be defined, and allows for distinctions between individual performances to be made. In addition, the procedures for investigating the reliability and aspects of the validity of norm-referenced scores are well established and well known. However, from an educational point of view its dependence on comparisons across a population has been seen as being inappropriately competitive, and discouraging for the 'average' student.

An alternative approach which does not use a comparison between individuals as its frame of reference is known as **criterion-referenced measurement**. Here, individual performances are evaluated against a verbal description of a satisfactory performance at a given level. In this way, a series of performance goals can be set for individual learners and they can reach these at their own rate. In this way, motivation is maintained, and the striving is for a 'personal best' rather than against other learners. Of course, even here comparison may creep in, as learners will compare the levels they and others have reached. Raters, too, will inevitably have in their heads a reference map of the range of achievement they have come to expect as teachers or raters, and locate the current performance accordingly. Nevertheless, in principle it is useful to distinguish the two broad approaches to assessment. Because criterion-referenced measurement involves evaluation of performance against descriptors, it typically involves judgement as to how a performance should be classified. Thus, measurement procedures used in criterion referenced approaches will include the indices of the quality of raters (inter-rater reliability indices, classification analysis, and so on) presented earlier in this chapter. Norm-referenced approaches require a score distribution, whose frequencies can be modelled in terms of the expected frequencies of the normal distribution. A score distribution implies the existence of a range of possible scores. Language tests which involve multiple items (and hence a range of possible total scores) generate such distributions, and so norm-referenced approaches are more typically associated with comprehension tests, or tests of grammar and vocabulary.

New approaches to measurement

New measurement approaches continually emerge. The most significant of them is known by the general name of **Item Response Theory** (**IRT**). IRT represents a new approach to item analysis (see earlier discussion). This, on the face of it, unexciting characteristic has important practical implications. It greatly facilitates the formerly very difficult business of **test equating** (producing tests of equivalent difficulty). It also permits **test linking**, that is, using tests of differing but known relative difficulty to measure the growth of individuals over time. IRT also makes possible the development of **computer adaptive tests**, a form of computer-delivered test to be discussed in detail in Chapter 8. IRT has also made great strides in the analysis of data from performance assessments, particularly through the branch of IRT known as **Rasch measurement**. Readers wishing to learn more about these new developments are referred to the suggestions for further reading in Section 3 (References).

Conclusion

In this chapter we have considered a number of ways in which concepts and practices from the field of educational measurement or psychometrics have had an impact on the area of language assessment. We distinguished different approaches to measurement, with different sets of assumptions, and some of the most common techniques associated with each for investigating the quality of language tests. We also drew attention to the new developments taking place in the field.

It has been argued recently that too obsessive a concern with measurement considerations can have a destructive effect educationally. For example, the move away from multiple-choice items in favour of assessment of integrated performances is in line with communicative approaches to language teaching and arguably therefore likely to have a beneficial impact on the curriculum and on classroom practice. But it is also more difficult to achieve acceptable levels of reliability in rater-mediated assessment than it is on multi-item multiple choice tests. Which consideration—validity or reliability—should predominate in such a case? This brings up one of the central issues in testing, namely that one might test what is readily testable rather than what needs to be tested to provide a proper assessment of language ability. And the question of what counts as proper assessment involves a consideration of the social and educational responsibility of language assessment. These are matters to be taken up in the following chapter.

7
The social character of language tests

Introduction

At a moment of dramatic intensity in the theatre, the glare of a single spotlight can isolate an individual actor from his or her surroundings. The spotlight focuses the spectator's attention on the psychological state of the character being portrayed. Temporarily at least, the surroundings, including other actors present, are rendered invisible for the audience. Until fairly recently, thinking about language assessment was like this. It focused exclusively on the skills and abilities of the individual being assessed. Educational assessment has traditionally drawn its concepts and procedures primarily from the field of psychology, and more specifically from the branch of psychology known as psychometrics, that is, the measurement of individual cognitive abilities. But what does the bright spotlight of this individualizing perspective exclude? What lies behind, around? Imagine the spotlight going off to be replaced by normal stage lighting: the other actors on the stage are revealed. Now imagine the performance continuing, but the house lights coming up, so that the audience is revealed. Imagine finally the side curtains being pulled back and the stage set removed to expose all the personnel working behind the scenes. The individual performance is now exposed as forming part of a larger collective activity, one which is deliberate, constructed for a particular purpose. It involve the efforts of many others in addition to the individual whose performance is 'in the spotlight'.

This chapter presents a perspective on assessment which focuses on the larger framing and social meaning of assessment. Such a perspective has drawn on diverse fields including sociology, political and cultural theory, and discourse analysis for its analytic tools and concepts, together with an expanded notion of test validity.

The institutional character of assessment

The individualized and individualizing focus of traditional approaches described so far is really rather surprising when we consider the inherently institutional character of assessment. When test reforms are introduced within the educational system, they are likely to figure prominently in the press and become matters of public concern. This is because they impinge directly on people's lives. When an assessment is made, it is not done by someone acting in a private capacity, motivated by personal curiosity about the other individual, but in an institutional role, and serving institutional purposes. These will typically involve the fulfilment of policy objectives in education and other areas of social policy. And social practice raises questions of social responsibility.

Assessment and social policy

Language tests have a long history of use as instruments of social and cultural exclusion. One of the earliest recorded instances is the shibboleth test, mentioned in the Old Testament. Following a decisive military battle between two neighbouring ethnic groups, members of the vanquished group attempted to escape by blending in with their culturally and linguistically very similar victors. The two groups spoke varieties of a single language and it was typically possible to distinguish between speakers of either variety by the way they pronounced words beginning with a sibilant sound. The victors pronounced such words with an [sh] sound, the vanquished with the sound [s]. So the word 'shibboleth' (meaning according to some authorities 'an ear of wheat', others 'a stream') was used as a single item language test by the victorious group in order to detect the enemy in their midst. Individuals suspected of being members of the vanquished were asked to say this word, and if they pronounced it 'sibboleth', they failed the test. In this case, failure was fatal since the test-takers were immediately put to death. Poor performance on a test may have serious consequences, though fortunately not usually as dire as this.

Notice that the test here is a test of authenticity of identity, rather than of proficiency; a single instance is enough to betray the identity which the test aims to detect. A more recent instance of a detection test is the proposal in the 1960s, but never implemented, for a language test to be used by the Royal Canadian Mounted Police to exclude homosexual recruits. Word lists which included some items of homosexual slang (words such as *camp*, *cruise*, *fruit*, and *trade*) would be presented to recruits, and the sweatiness of their palms (a sign of nervousness) would be measured electrically. It was assumed that only homosexuals familiar with the subculture in which these terms were used, with secondary slang meanings, would recognize and respond to the ambiguity of the terms. They would become nervous, sweat, and be detected. In this test, a perfect score was zero!

More conventional proficiency tests have also been used for purposes of exclusion. Prior to the Second World War the Australian Government used a language test as part of their policy to exclude immigrants other than those coming from the British Isles. Those applying to immigrate could be administered a dictation test in any language selected by the immigration officer. If the person passed the test in English, then any one of a range of other languages could be used until the candidate failed. In one notorious case, a Hungarian Jewish refugee from Hitler's persecutions applied for immigrant status. He was a polyglot and passed the test in a number of languages before finally failing in Gaelic, thereby being refused entry and thus facing a tragic fate in Europe. The blatancy of such a practice is not readily replicated elsewhere, but it illustrates the possibility that language tests can form part of a politically and morally objectionable policy.

Assessment and educational policy

Assessment serves policy functions in educational contexts, too. One example is in the area of vocational education and training for adults. Most industrialized countries have, in recent years, responded to the need for the upgrading of the workforce in the face of rapid technological change by developing more flexible policies for the recognition and certification of specific work-related skills, each of which may be termed a **competency**. National competency frameworks, consisting of an ordered series of 'can do' statements describing levels of performance on relevant job-related tasks, have been adopted. Language and literacy competency frameworks have been developed as part of these policies.

In international education, tests are used to control access to educational opportunities. Typically, international students need to meet a standard on a test of language for academic purposes before they are admitted to the university of their choice. Is this reasonable? Should access to educational opportunity be restricted on the basis of a language test? If it is agreed that some assessment of language ability is reasonable in this context, then questions arise regarding the level of proficiency to be required, and how this should be determined. Further, should the assessment of language proficiency be carried out within the context of performance on typical academic tasks? But then, does this not mean that those who have had some experience of such tasks have the advantage over those who do not? If this is so, then one might question the fairness of such tasks as instruments for the testing of language ability. One can also raise the question of how native speakers might perform on such integrated tasks, and why, given that they are admitted to the same courses of study, they should not also be required to subject themselves to assessment.

The social responsibility of the language tester

The policies and practices discussed in the preceding two sections throw up a host of questions about fairness, and about the policy issues surrounding testing practice. They also raise the question of the responsibilities of language testers. Recently, serious attention has been given to these issues for the first time, an overdue development, one might say, given the essentially institutional character of testing.

Imagine the following situation involving the use of language tests within immigration policy. You live in an English-speaking country which accepts substantial numbers of new settlers each year. The current immigration policy distinguishes between categories of intending settlers. The claims of refugees are privileged in various ways, as are those of family members of local citizens (settled immigrants have the right to apply to bring into the country parents who are living in the country of origin). English language proficiency and knowledge of local cultural practices have not been a criterion in selection in such cases. A further category of individuals with no prior connection to the country, and who are not refugees, may also apply for immigration; but the selection process for them is much tougher—approximately only one in ten who apply is granted permission to settle. Selection criteria for this category of applicants include educational level, type of work expertise, age, and proficiency in English, among other things. English language proficiency is currently assessed informally by an immigration officer at the time of interview. The immigration authorities approach you to be part of a team commissioned with the development of a specific test for the purpose of more accurately determining the proficiency of intending immigrants in this category. What ethical issues do you face?

On the one hand, the advent of the new test might appear to promote fairness. Obviously, as judgements in the current informal procedures are not made by trained language evaluators, and no quality control procedures are in place, there are inconsistencies in standards, and hence unfairness to individuals. A carefully constructed test, both more relevant in its content, and more reliable in its decisions, appears on the face of it to be fairer for the majority. On the other hand, the introduction of such an instrument raises worrying possibilities. Might not the authorities, once it is in place, be tempted to use it on previously exempt categories, for example refugees or family members? Who will be in charge of interpreting scores on the test? Who will set **cut-scores** for 'passing' and 'failing'? In response to your inquiries on this point, you are informed that cut-scores will vary according to the requirements of immigration policy, higher when there is political pressure to restrict immigration numbers, lower when there is a labour shortage and immigrant numbers are set to rise. The political nature of the test is revealed by such facts—where does that leave you as a socially responsible test developer? Should you refuse to get involved?

Such cases raise issues of the ethics of language testing practice, which are becoming a matter of considerable current debate. We can distinguish two views, both of which acknowledge the social and political role of tests. One holds that language testing practice can be made ethical, and stresses the individual responsibility of testers to ensure that they are. The other sees tests as essentially sociopolitical constructs, which, since they are designed as instruments of power and control, must therefore be subjected to the same kind of critique as are all other political structures in society. We may refer to the first view as **ethical language testing**; the latter is usually termed **critical language testing**.

Ethical language testing

Those who argue that language testing can be an ethical activity take either a broader or more restricted view of the ethics of testing. We can call the former the social responsibility view, the latter the traditional view.

Those who advocate the position of socially responsible language testing reject the view that language testing is merely a scientific and technical activity. They appeal to recent developments in thinking about validity, especially to the notion of consequential validity. In general, this means that evaluation of a test's validity needs to take into account the wanted and unwanted consequences that follow from the introduction of the test. Some take the view that consequential validity, like validity of other kinds (as discussed in Chapter 5), is the responsibility of the test developer and needs to be taken into account, not only by anticipating possible consequences in test design, but also by monitoring its effects in implementation.

Generally, this expanded sense of responsibility sees ethical testing practice as involving test developers in taking responsibility for the effects of tests. There are three main areas of concern here. One of these is **accountability**. This has to do with a sense of responsibility to the people most immediately affected by the test, principally the test-takers, but also those who will use the information it provides. The test (and hence the test developer) need to be accountable to them. A second area relates to the influence that testing has on teaching, the so-called **washback** effect. The third involves a consideration of the effect of a test beyond the classroom, the ripples or waves it makes in the wider educational and social world: what we can call the test **impact**.

Accountability

Ethical testing practice is seen as involving making tests accountable to test-takers. Test developers are typically more preoccupied with satisfying the demands of those commissioning the test, and with their own work of creating a workable test. Test-takers are seldom represented on **test development committees** which supervise the work of test development, and represent the interests of stakeholders. Minimally, accountability would require test developers to provide test-takers with complete information on what is expected of them in the test. Such information is often provided in the form of a **test users' handbook** or **manual**, which provides information on the rationale for the test and its structure, general information on its content, and the format of items, and sample items.

More substantially, test developers should be required to demonstrate that the test content and format are relevant to candidates, and that the testing practice is accountable to their needs and interests. Too often, traditional testing procedures and formats may be preferred even in situations where they are no longer relevant. For example, British examinations originally developed for the British secondary school system are still used in Africa, despite the inappropriateness of their content and format.

An aspect of accountability is the question of determining the norms of language behaviour which will act as a reference point in the assessment. This will include issues such as the appropriate variety of the language to be tested. In an era where no single variety of English constitutes a norm everywhere, the question arises of how much of the variation among English speakers it is appropriate to include in a test.

Consider, for example, the **TOEFL** test, used primarily for selection of international students to universities in the United States. Given the diversity of varieties of English, both native and nonnative, typically encountered in the academic environment there, it might be argued that it is responsible to include examples of those varieties in the test rather than to include only samples of the standard variety.

Washback

The power of tests in determining the life chances of individuals and in influencing the reputation of teachers and schools means that they can have a strong influence on the curriculum. The effect of tests on teaching and learning is known as test **washback**.

Ethical language testing practice, it is felt, should work to ensure positive washback from tests.

For example, it is sometimes argued that performance assessments have better washback than multiple choice test formats or other individual item formats, such as cloze, which focus on isolated elements of knowledge or skill. As performance assessments required integration of knowledge and skills in performance on realistic tasks, preparation for such assessments will presumably encourage teachers and students to spend time engaged in performance of such tasks as part of the teaching. In contrast, multiple choice format item tests of knowledge of grammar or vocabulary may inhibit communicative approaches to learning and teaching.

Authorities responsible for assessment sometimes use assessment reform to drive curriculum reform, believing that the assessment can be designed to have positive washback on the curriculum. However, research both on the presumed negative washback of conservative test formats, and on the presumed positive washback of communicative assessment (assumed to be more progressive) has shown that washback is often rather unpredictable. Whether or not the desired effect is achieved will depend on local conditions in classrooms, the established traditions of teaching, the immediate motivation of learners, and the frequently unpredictable ways in which classroom interactions develop. These can only be established after the event, post hoc, on the basis of information collected once the reform has been introduced.

Test impact

Tests can also have effects beyond the classroom. The wider effect of tests on the community as a whole, including the school, is referred to as test **impact**. For example, the existence of tests such as TOEFL, used as gatekeeping mechanisms for international education, and administered to huge numbers of candidates all over the world, has effects beyond the classroom, in terms of educational policy and the allocation of resources to education. In certain areas of the world, university selection is based directly on performance in the assessments of the senior year of high school. This has often led to the existence of tightly controlled formal examinations, partly in order to make what tended to become a very competitive assessment as psychometrically reliable as possible. However, in an era where most students are completing a secondary education, such an assessment no longer meets the needs of the majority of students. A curriculum and assessment reform in favour of continuous assessment and the completion of projects and assignments in such a case would have widespread impact on families, universities, employers, and employment and welfare services. In fact, in one such case, part of the impact of the reform was to open the door to abuses of the assessment process by wealthy families, who could afford to hire private tutors to coach their children through the projects they had to complete in order to gain the scores they needed to enter the university of their choice. Test impact is likely to be complex and unpredictable.

Codes of professional ethics for language testers

In contrast to those advocating the direct social responsibility of the tester, a more traditional approach involves limiting the social responsibility of language testers to questions of the professional ethics of their practice. In this view, the approach to the ethics of language testing practice should be the same as that taken within other areas of professional practice, such as medicine or law. Professional bodies of language testers should formulate codes of practice which will guide language testers in their work. The emphasis is on good professional practice: that is, language testers should in general take responsibility for the development of quality language tests. The larger questions of the politics of language testing fall not so much within the domain of the ethics of language testing practice as such; instead they represent the ethical questions that all citizens must face—for example, on issues such as capital punishment, abortion and the like.

Those taking this view understand consequential validity as concerning consequential impediments to the interpretability of test scores. For example, in the case of the notorious Australian dictation test discussed earlier, test developers were presumably aware of the uses to which the test was to be put. But instead of arguing that language testers have an ethical responsibility to object to the policy behind the test in such a case, it may be sufficient (and arguably more effective) to oppose the test on the basis of professional validity arguments. What is wrong with this test is that there was only one acceptable inference possible from the test: that the test-taker was unsuitable for acceptance into Australia. Proficiency in the range of languages tested was not relevant to the question of the person's suitability for settlement in Australia. The problem with the test, in this view, is that the test construct is not meaningful or interpretable in this context. It is not a valid test. The fact that it constitutes an offence against social justice thus does not need to be addressed directly; rather, the test is found wanting within an expanded theory of validity, that is, one which includes consequential validity.

Critical language testing

A much more radical view of the social and political role of tests is being formulated as part of the developing area known as critical applied linguistics. This applies current social theory and critical theory to issues within applied linguistics generally. Language testing, as a quintessentially institutional activity, is facing increasing scrutiny from this perspective. The basic tenets of such a view are that the principles and practices that have become established as common sense or common knowledge are actually ideologically loaded to favour those in power, and so need to be exposed as an imposition on the powerless. In this view, there would be little point in tinkering with existing institutional constructs, working within the framework they determine. What is needed is a radical reconstruction which changes the whole ideological foundations. In this perspective the very concept of testing, of language or anything else, gets redefined in socio-political terms. Critical language testing is best understood as an intellectual project to expose the role of tests in this exercise of power. For example, the existence of language testing on a huge international scale—what some have called industrialized language testing—is ripe for critical analysis. There are hundreds of thousands of individual administrations of the TOEFL test in any year, in a huge number of countries; what are we to make of this phenomenon in critical terms?

From the perspective of critical language testing, the emphasis in ethical language testing on the individual responsibility of the language tester is misguided because it presupposes that this would operate within the established institution of testing, and so essentially accept the status quo and concede its legitimacy. Critical language testing at its most radical is not reformist since reform is a matter of modification not total replacement. At its most radical indeed, it would not recognize testing as we know it at all. Given this, it is perhaps unsurprising that language testers themselves have found it difficult to articulate this critique, or have interpreted it as implying the necessity for individual ethically responsible behaviour on the part of testers. The critique, if and when it comes, may emerge most forcefully from outside the field. Given the disciplinary borders of knowledge and influence in the field, however, any criticism from outside may be heard only with difficulty by practitioners within.

Conclusion

In this chapter we have examined the institutional character of tests and the implications of this for understanding the nature of language testing as a social practice, and the responsibility of language testers. Language testing, like language itself, cannot ultimately be isolated from wider social and political implications. It is perhaps not surprising after all that the field has only belatedly grasped this fact, and even now is uncertain about the extent to which it is able or willing to articulate a thorough critique of its practices. This may best be left to those not involved in language testing. Language testers themselves meanwhile stand to benefit from a greater awareness of language testing as a social practice. It may lead to a more responsible exercise of the power of tests, and a more deeply questioning approach to the questions of test score meaning which lie at the heart of the validity of language tests.

8
New directions—and dilemmas?

We live in a time of contradictions. The speed and impressiveness of technological advance suggest an era of great certainty and confidence. Yet at the same time current social theories undermine our certainties, and have engendered a profound questioning of existing assumptions about the self and its social construction. Aspects of these contradictory trends also define important points of change in language testing. The applications of technological innovations in language testing remain for the most part rooted in traditional modernist assumptions about the nature of performance and the possibilities of measurement of language ability. It is assumed, for example, that there is such a thing as 'ability' which is located in the mind of the candidate, which is, as it were, projected directly in performance; that the individual candidate is solely responsible for his/her performance in the test; and that ability can be measured more or less objectively. But it is these very individualizing modernist assumptions of testing practice which are now being challenged by new theories of performance. Language testing is a field in crisis, one which is masked by the impressive appearance of technological advance.

Computers and language testing

Rapid developments in computer technology have had a major impact on test delivery. Already, many important national and international language tests, including TOEFL, are moving to **computer based testing** (**CBT**). Stimulus texts and prompts are presented not in examination booklets but on the screen, with candidates being required to key in their responses. The advent of CBT has not necessarily involved any change in the test content, which may remain quite conservative in its assumptions, but often simply represents a change in test method.

The proponents of computer based testing can point to a number of advantages. First, scoring of fixed response items can be done automatically, and the candidate can be given a score immediately. Second, the computer can deliver tests that are tailored to the particular abilities of the candidate. It seems inefficient for all candidates to take all the questions on a test; clearly some are so easy for some candidates that they provide little information on their abilities; others are too hard to be of use. It makes sense to use the very limited time available for testing to focus on those items that are just within, and just beyond a candidate's threshold of ability.

Computer adaptive tests do just this. At the beginning of the test, a small number of common items are presented to all candidates. Depending on how an individual candidate performs on those items, he/she is subsequently presented only with items estimated to be within his/her likely ability range. The computer updates its estimate of the candidate's ability after each response. In this way, the test adapts itself to the candidate. Such tests require the prior creation of an **item bank**, a large group of items which have been thoroughly trialled, and whose likely difficulty for candidates at given levels of ability has been estimated as precisely as possible.

Items are drawn from the item bank in response to the performance of the candidate on each item, until a point where a stable and precise estimate of the candidate's ability is achieved. In this way each candidate will receive a test consisting of a possibly unique combination of items from the bank, a test suited precisely to the candidate's ability. The existence of large item banks makes possible a third advantage of computer based testing. Tests can be provided on demand, because so many item combinations are possible that test security is not compromised. Computer adaptive tests of grammar and vocabulary have long been available, but recently similar tests of listening and reading skills have been developed.

The use of computers for the delivery of test materials raises questions of validity, as we might expect. For example, different levels of familiarity with computers will affect people's performance with them, and interaction with the computer may be a stressful experience for some. Attempts are usually made to reduce the impact of prior experience by the provision of an extensive tutorial on relevant skills as part of the test (that is, before the test proper begins). Nevertheless, the question about the impact of computer delivery still remains.

Questions about the importance of different kinds of presentation format are raised or exacerbated by the use of computers. In a writing test, the written product will appear in typeface and will not be handwritten; in a reading test, the text to be read will appear on a screen, not on paper. Do raters react differentially to printed versus handwritten texts? Is any inference we might draw about a person's ability to read texts presented on computer screens generalizable to that person's ability to read texts printed on paper, and vice versa? In computerized tests of written composition, composing processes are likely to be different, because of word processing capacities available on the computer. Do such differences in aspects of test method result in different conclusions about a candidate's ability? A complex programme of research is needed to answer these questions.

The ability of computers to carry out various kinds of automatic processes on spoken or written texts is having an impact on testing. These will include the ability to do rapid counts of the number of tokens of individual words, to analyse the grammar of sentences, to count pauses, to calculate the range of vocabulary, and to analyse features of pronunciation. Already these automatic measures of pronunciation or writing quality are being used in place of a second human rating of performances, and have been found to contribute as much to overall reliability as a human rating. Of course, such computer operations have limitations. For example, in the testing of speaking, they are bound to be better at acoustic than auditory aspects of pronunciation, and cannot readily identify intelligibility since this is a function of unpredictable contextual factors. Nevertheless, we can expect many further rapid advances in these fields, with direct application to testing.

Technology and the testing of speaking

While computers represent the most rapid point of technological change, other less complex technologies, which have been in use for some time, have led to similar validity questions.

Tape recorders can be used in the administration of speaking tests. Candidates are presented with a prompt on tape, and are asked to respond as if they were talking to a person, the response being recorded on tape. This performance is then scored from the tape. Such a test is called a **semi-direct test** of speaking, as compared with a direct test format such as a live face-to-face interview.

But not everybody likes speaking to tapes! We all know the difficulty many people experience in leaving messages on answering machines. Most test-takers prefer a direct rather than a semi-direct format if given the formats. But the question then arises as to whether these options are equivalent in testing terms. How far can you infer the same ability from performance on different formats? It is possible for somebody to be voluble in direct face-to-face interaction but tongue-tied when confronted with a machine, and vice versa. Research looking at the performance of the same candidates under each condition has shown that this is a complex issue, as not all candidates react in the same way (hardly surprising, of course). Some candidates prefer the tape, some prefer a live interlocutor, and performance generally improves in the condition that is preferred. But we must also add the interlocutor factor. Some candidates get on well with particular interlocutors, others are inhibited by them. And there is the rater factor. Some raters react negatively to tapes, and to particular interlocutors, and may, without realizing it, either compensate or 'punish' the candidate when giving their ratings.

Given such issues, why are semi-direct tests used? Cost considerations and the logistics of mass test administration are likely to favour their use.

The semi-direct format is cheaper to administer, as a live interlocutor (the person who interacts with the candidate) does not have to be provided. On the other hand, the fact that the tape still has to be individually rated means that the test is by no means inexpensive; and in many face-to-face speaking tests the interlocutor and the rater are the same person, so that no real saving is achieved. In addition, the preparation of the tape and the supply of recording equipment is expensive. Nevertheless, in appropriate circumstances, considerable economies can be achieved. A further advantage is that in cases of languages where there are only a small number of candidates presenting for assessment at any one time, testing can be provided virtually on demand in any location. This would not be possible if a trained interlocutor for that language had to be found. Finally, research has demonstrated that the interlocutor you interact with may affect your score. Some interlocutors elicit performances which trigger a favourable impression of the candidate; others have the reverse effect. The problem is that raters typically don't realize that it is the interlocutor's behaviour which is contributing to the impression generated—a classic case of 'blame the victim'. As a semi-direct test removes the interlocutor variable—all candidates face the same prompt, delivered by tape—it might be felt that the semi-direct test has the potential to be a fairer test.

The issues raised by semi-direct tests of speaking are rapidly becoming more urgent as pressure to make tests more communicative leads to an increased demand for speaking tests. But such tests can often only feasibly be provided in a semi-direct format, given huge numbers of candidates sitting for the test in a large number of countries worldwide, as for example with a test such as TOEFL. The issue here is a fundamental one. It illustrates the tension between the feasibility of tests (the need to design and administer them practically and cheaply if they are to be of any use at all), and their validity. There are three basic critical dimensions of tests (validity, reliability, and feasibility) whose demands need to be balanced. The right balance will depend on the test context and test purpose.

Dilemmas: whose performance?

The speed of technological advances affecting language testing sometimes gives an impression of a field confidently moving ahead, notwithstanding the issues of validity raised above. But concomitantly the change in perspective from the individual to the social nature of test performance has provoked something of an intellectual crisis in the field. In Chapter 7 we looked at the social nature of test performance in a larger political and cultural sense; here will examine the social character of performance at a more micro level, at the level of interaction. Developments in discourse analysis and pragmatics have revealed the essential interactivity of all communication. This is especially clear in relation to the assessment of speaking. The problem is that of isolating the contribution of a single individual (the candidate) in a joint communicative activity. As soon as you try to test use (as opposed to usage) you cannot confine yourself to the single individual. So whose performance are we assessing?

Take the following example. A Thai nurse working with elderly patients in an American geriatric hospital setting is liked and respected by her patients and supervising colleagues, and is effective in her work despite glaring deficiencies in her grammar, vocabulary and pronunciation in English. The people she communicates with expect to have to take some responsibility for the success of the communication, in view of her limited English proficiency. They contribute through the active process of drawing inferences from what she has said, checking that they have understood, and seeking clarification in various ways. All of these activities on their part contribute to successful communication with her. Her professional knowledge of nursing is excellent, and this helps in the framing of her communication, to make it relevant. With her professional competence, pleasant personality, and the need for her interlocutors to communicate with her, clinical communication seems to be successful; there is no reason to exclude her from the workplace, even though this might be suggested by a 'cold' assessment of her communication in the absence of an interlocutor, and in non-clinical contexts.

A contrasting example. A nurse from Hong Kong, a native speaker of Cantonese and a competent speaker of English by most standards, is at the centre of a controversy in a hospital in an English-speaking country. A sudden emergency with a patient in the ward requires the nurse to make a telephone call to the receptionist, a native speaker of English, for urgent help. The receptionist claims not to be able to understand the nurse, the message does not get through, and the patient dies. It turns out that the receptionist has a reputation for being racist. It is possible that she in a sense refused to understand? Whatever the explanation, communication did not take place. Whom should we blame for this breakdown?

In each of these examples, it is not clear who is responsible for the success or failure of the communication. It seems that success or failure is a joint achievement: the communication is a co-

construction. In assessment, should we not then take the interlocutor into account in our predictions of successful communication? But how can that be done? And how can this be made to fit the institutional need for a score about individual candidates on their own, not about individuals and their interlocutors? Is proficiency best understood as something that individuals carry round in their heads with them, or does it only exist in actual performances, which are never solo? Note that the issue of the joint responsibility for communication raised here relates not only to communication involving non-native speakers; it is equally relevant for communication between native speakers. What is at issue here are general pragmatic conditions of normal communication, and the difficulty of pinning them down in any testing procedure. This is then another fundamental dilemma for language testing.

The issues raised here show the way in which language testing, as in other fields of assessment, is crucially dependent on definitions of the test construct. It is thus, in a way, vulnerable to our evolving understanding of language and communication, and cannot be protected by its success in other aspects, for example advances in the technical aspects of psychometrics or in the technology of assessment. The disconcerting aspect of the current situation is that a growing loss of confidence in the possibility or even desirability of locating competence in the individual, as illustrated in the examples presented above, seems to challenge the very adequacy of our current theories of measurement, with their promise of providing a single summary score as the basis for the reliable classification decision that we seek. Instead of the individual carrying a measurable proficiency round in his or her head, we have a multiplicity of selves in interaction in a multiplicity of interactional contexts. How can measurement do justice to this? And in the dazzle of technological advance, we may need a continuing reminder of the nature of communication as a shared human activity, and that the idea that one of the participants can be replaced by a machine is really a technological fantasy.

Language testing remains a complex and perplexing activity. While insights from evolving theories of communication may be disconcerting, it is necessary to fully grasp them and the challenge they pose if our assessments are to have any chance of having the meaning we intend them to have. Language testing is an uncertain and approximate business at the best of times, even if to the outsider this may be camouflaged by its impressive, even daunting, technical (and technological) trappings, not to mention the authority of the institutions whose goals tests serve. Every test is vulnerable to good questions, about language and language use, about measurement, about test procedures, and about the uses to which the information in tests is to be put. In particular, a language test is only as good as the theory of language on which it is based, and it is within this area of theoretical inquiry into the essential nature of language and communication that we need to develop our ability to ask the next question. And the next.

SECTION 2
Readings

Chapter 1
Testing, testing . . . What is a language test?

Text 1

ALAN DAVIES: 'The construction of language tests' in
J.P.B. Allen and Alan Davies (eds.): *The Edinburgh Course
in Applied Linguistics Volume 4: Testing and Experimental
Methods*. Oxford University Press 1977, pages 45–46

*In this paper, Davies distinguishes four important uses or
functions of language tests: achievement, proficiency, apti-
tude, and diagnostic. In this extract he discusses the first two
of these.*

Achievement

Achievement or attainment tests are concerned with assessing
what has been learned of a known syllabus. This may be within a
school or within a total educational system. Thus the typical
external school examinations ('Ordinary' level or 'Advanced'
level in England, 'Highers' in Scotland), the university degree
exams and so on are all examples of achievement tests. The use
being made of the measure is to find out just how much has been
learned of what has been taught (i.e., of the syllabus).
Achievement type tests end there. Although the primary interest is
in the past, i.e. what has been learned, very often some further use
is made of the same test in order to make meaningful decisions
about the pupils' future. It would, presumably, be possible to be
interested entirely in the past of the pupils; Carroll's 'meaningful

decisions' then would refer to the syllabus, i.e., to any necessary alterations to it that might be necessary or to the teaching method to be used for the next group of students. But achievement tests are almost always used for other purposes as well. It is important to recognize this and to account for it in one's test construction. But, as will be maintained later under validity, this is essentially a function of the syllabus. All that an achievement test can do is to indicate how much of a syllabus has been learned; it cannot make predictions as to pupils' future performance unless the syllabus has been expressly designed for this purpose.

▷ *What are some of the functions of the examinations Davies mentions (external school examinations, university degree examinations) other than looking back over what has been learned?*

▷ *What 'future performance' does the writer have in mind? In what way can the design of a syllabus be used as the basis for predictions as to pupils' future performance?*

Proficiency

Proficiency tests, as we see it, are concerned with assessing what has been learned of a known or an unknown syllabus. Here we see the distinction between proficiency and achievement. In the non-language field we might consider, say, a driving tests as a kind of proficiency test since there is the desire to apply a common standard to all who present themselves whatever their previous driving experience, over which of course there has been no control at all. In the language field there are several well-known proficiency exams of the same journeyman kind: the Cambridge Proficiency Exams, the Michigan Tests, the Test of English as a Foreign Language (TOEFL) and English Proficiency Test Battery (EPTB). These all imply that a common standard is being applied to all comers. More sophisticated proficiency tests (more sophisticated in use, not in design) may be constructed as research tools to determine just how much control over a language is needed for certain purposes, for example medical studies in a second language.

▷ *How does the fact that a proficiency test may relate to an unknown syllabus serve as the basis for a distinction from achievement tests?*

> If syllabus content is absent as a basis for the content of a proficiency test, how can we decide what it should contain?

Chapter 2
Communication and the design of language tests

Text 2
ROBERT LADO: *Language Testing: The Construction and Use of Foreign Language Tests.* Longmans 1961, pages 22–24

Lado presents the case for basing language tests on a theory of language description and a theory of learning, in particular on the points of structural contrast between the learner's first language and the target language. His recommendations about testing dominated practice for nearly twenty years, and are still influential in powerful tests such as TOEFL.

The theory of language testing assumes that language is a system of habits of communication. These habits permit the communicant to give his conscious attention to the over-all meaning he is conveying or perceiving. These habits involve matters of form, meaning and distribution at several levels of structure, namely those of the sentence, clause, phrase, word, morpheme and phoneme. Within these levels are structures of modification, sequence, parts of sentences. Below them are habits of articulation, syllable type, and collocations. Associated with them and sometimes part of them are patterns of intonation, stress and rhythm. ...

The individual is not aware that so much of what he does in using language is done through a complex system of habits. When he attempts to communicate in a foreign language that he knows partially, he adopts the same linguistic posture as when using his native language. He thinks of the over-all meaning and proceeds to encode it in the linguistic forms of the foreign language. He may concentrate consciously in addition on one or another matter of grammar or pronunciation or vocabulary, but the bulk of the encoding goes to his habit system and here it is channeled through the system of habits of his native language. This in psychology is known as transfer. He transfers the habit systems of his native language to the foreign tongue. ...

When this transfer occurs, some of the units and patterns transferred will function satisfactorily in the foreign language and will not constitute a learning problem. Other units and patterns will not function satisfactorily in the foreign language. Against these the student will have to learn the new units and patterns. These constitute the real learning problems.

These learning problems turn out to be matters of form, meaning, distribution, or a combination of these. They can be predicted and described in most cases by a systematic linguistic comparison of the two language structures. ...

The theory assumes that testing control of the problems is testing control of the language. Problems are those units and patterns which do not have a counterpart in the native language or that have counterparts with structurally different distribution or meaning.

▷ *In what terms does Lado describe knowledge of language? Give some examples of the kinds of knowledge he means.*

▷ *In situations where the test population is drawn from learners of diverse linguistic background, what problems would arise in practice if you based the design of language tests on contrasts between the language being tested and the language of the test takers? How might one get around this difficulty?*

Text 3

BERNARD SPOLSKY: 'Introduction: Linguists and language testers' in B. Spolsky (ed.): *Approaches to Language Testing.* [*Advances in Language Testing Series: 2*] Center for Applied Linguistics 1978, pages v–vi

Spolsky distinguishes three historical periods of modern language testing up to the time of his writing: the pre-scientific, the psychometric-structuralist, and the integrative-sociolinguistic. He discusses the first two of these in this extract.

The pre-scientific period (or trend, for it still holds sway in many parts of the world) may be characterized by a lack of concern for statistical matters or for such notions as objectivity or reliability.

In its simplest form, it assumes that one can and must rely completely on the judgment of an experienced teacher, who can tell after a few minutes' conversation, or after reading a student's essay, what mark to give. In the pre-scientific mode, oral examinations of any kind were the exception: language testing was assumed to be a matter of open-ended written examination. ...

The next period, however, sees the invasion of the field by experts. The psychometric-structuralist trend, though hyphenated for reasons that will become apparent, is marked by the interaction (and conflict) of two sets of experts, agreeing with each other mainly in their belief that testing can be made precise, objective, reliable, and scientific. The first of these groups of experts were the testers, the psychologists responsible for the development of modern theories and techniques of educational measurement. Their key concerns have been to provide "objective" measures using various statistical techniques to assure reliability and certain kinds of validity. ...

The better known work of the testers was the development of short item, multiple choice, "objective" tests. The demands of statistical measures of reliability and validity were seen as of paramount importance...

There were two results from this emphasis. First, tests like this required written response, and so were limited to reading and listening. Second, the items chosen did not reflect newer ideas about language teaching and learning. ...

The second major impetus of the "scientific" period, or approach, then, was when a new set of experts added notions from the science of language to those from the science of educational measurement...

There was at the time still an easy congruence between American structuralist views of language and the psychological theories and practical needs of testers. On the theoretical side, both agreed that knowledge of language was a matter of habits; on the practical side, testers wanted, and structuralists knew how to deliver, long lists of small items which could be sampled and tested objectively. The structural linguist's view of language as essentially a matter of item-and-arrangement fell easily into the tester's notion of a set of discrete skills to be measured. ...

The marriage of the two fields, then, provided the basis for the flourishing of the standardized language test, with its special emphasis on ... the 'discrete structure point' item.

▷ *Spolsky implies that one of the implications of the transition between the two periods he describes was a transfer of the primary responsibility for tests from language teachers to testing experts in applied linguistics. What are the potential advantages and disadvantages of such a transfer?*

▷ *Spolsky argues that structuralist linguistics contributed to tests which featured 'discrete structure point' items. Look back at the material by Lado in Text 2 and suggest what the content of such items might be.*

Text 4

JOHN W. OLLER: *Language Tests at School.*
Longman 1979, pages 38–39

In this passage, Oller attempts to define language tests not in terms of the elements of knowledge to be tested, but in terms of the language processing operations required of learners. He makes a sharp distinction between what he calls pragmatic tests and the older tradition of discrete point tests associated with the work of Lado and which were the hallmark of tests within the psychometric-structuralist tradition.

It is possible to be somewhat more precise in saying what a pragmatic test is: it is any procedure or task that causes the learner to process sequences of elements in a language that conform to the normal contextual constraints of that language and which requires the learner to relate sequences of linguistic elements via pragmatic mapping to extralinguistic context. ...

In order for a test to say something meaningful (valid) about the efficiency of a learner's developing grammatical system, the pragmatic naturalness criteria require that the test invoke and challenge that developing grammatical system. This requires processing sequences of elements in the target language (even if it is the learner's first and only language) subject to temporal contextual constraints. In addition, the tasks must be such that for examinees to do them, linguistic sequences must be related to extralinguistic contexts in meaningful ways.

Examples of tasks that do not qualify as pragmatic tests include all discrete point tests, the rote recital of sequences of material without attention to meaning; the manipulation of sequences of verbal elements, possibly in complex ways, but in ways that do not require awareness of meaning. In brief, if the task does not require attention to meaning in temporally constrained sequences of linguistic elements, it cannot be construed as a pragmatic language test. Moreover, the constraints must be of the type that are found in normal use of the language, not merely in some classroom setting.... .

▷ *What does Oller mean, do you think, when he speaks of the normal constraints operating in relation to the use of language? How can these be reproduced in the test setting?*

▷ *Oller lists examples of tests which he would not classify as pragmatic tests. Give examples of tests that Oller would classify as pragmatic tests, i.e. that meet the requirements he sets down for such tests.*

Text 5

MICHAEL CANALE and MERRILL SWAIN: 'Theoretical bases of communicative approaches to second language teaching and testing' in *Applied Linguistics* 1, 1980, pages 28–30

In one of the most-cited discussions in applied linguistics, Canale and Swain apply the insights of Hymes to formulate a model of communicative competence for second language contexts, introducing the important notions of sociolinguistic and strategic competence in a second language.

Our own tentative theory of communicative competence minimally includes three main competencies: grammatical competence, sociolinguistic competence, and strategic competence. ...

Grammatical competence. This type of competence will be understood to include knowledge of lexical items and of rules of morphology, syntax, sentence-grammar semantics, and phonology. ...

Sociolinguistic competence. This component is made up of two sets of rules: sociocultural rules of use and rules of discourse.

Knowledge of these rules will be crucial in interpreting utterances for social meaning, particularly when there is a low level of transparency between the literal meaning of an utterance and the speaker's intention.

Sociocultural rules of use will specify the ways in which utterances are produced and understood appropriately with respect to the components of communicative events outlined by Hymes.... .

Until more clear-cut theoretical statements about rules of discourse emerge, it is perhaps most useful to think of these rules in terms of the cohesion (i.e. grammatical links) and coherence (i.e. appropriate combination of communicative functions) of groups of utterances.... .

Strategic competence. This component will be made up of verbal and non-verbal communication strategies that may be called into action to compensate for breakdowns in communication due to performance variables or to insufficient competence. Such strategies will be of two main types: those that relate primarily to grammatical competence (e.g. how to paraphrase grammatical forms that one has not mastered or cannot recall momentarily) and those that relate more to sociolinguistic competence (e.g. various role-playing strategies, how to address strangers when unsure of their social status).

▷ *Give examples of contexts where sociolinguistic competence could assume special importance, and therefore would be a particular focus of assessment.*

▷ *Canale and Swain do not refer to methods of assessment, only to the content or focus of assessment. In what different ways might you assess sociolinguistic competence?*

▷ *In what ways does strategic competence involve the learner's confidence or preparedness to take risks, which we might argue are features of his/her personality? Is strategic competence applicable to first language communication? If it is, does it transfer from first language to second language? How can strategic competence be evaluated?*

Chapter 3
The testing cycle

Text 6

LYLE F. BACHMAN: *Fundamental Considerations in Language Testing.* Oxford University Press 1990, pages 244–245

Bachman discusses two aspects of the validity of tests associated with test content: how relevant the test content is to the criterion situation, both in terms of the stimulus texts and the responses required of candidates; and how adequate a sample of criterion behaviour it is.

One of the first characteristics of a test that we, as prospective test users, examine is its content. If we cannot examine an actual copy of the test, we would generally like to see a table of specifications and example items, or at least a listing of the content areas covered, and the number of items, or relative importance of each area. Likewise, in developing a test, we begin with a definition of the content or ability domain, or at the very least, the list of content areas, from which we generate items, or test tasks. The consideration of test content is thus an important part of both test development and test use. *Demonstrating* that a test is relevant to and covers a given area of content or ability is therefore a necessary part of validation.

There are two aspects to this part of validation: *content relevance* and *content coverage*. The investigation of *content relevance* requires 'the specification of the behavioral domain in question and the attendant specification of the task or test domain' (Messick 1980: 1017). While it is generally recognized that this involves the specification of the ability domain, what is often ignored is that examining content relevance also requires the specification of the test method ...

▷ *'We begin with a definition of the content or ability domain': in your own words, and using tests with which you are familiar, give brief informal definitions of the content or ability domain on which the test content is based.*

▷ *How can the test methods form part of the content of the test?*

Give examples of test methods which would on the face of it be appropriate or inappropriate for a given domain.

The second aspect of examining test content is that of *content coverage*, or the extent to which the tasks required in the test adequately represent the behavioral domain in question. . . .

The problem with language tests, of course, is that we seldom have a domain definition that clearly and unambiguously identifies the set of language use tasks from which possible test tasks can be sampled, so that demonstrating either content relevance or content coverage is difficult.

▷ *What makes it difficult to specify the domain of language tests?*

Text 7

SANDRA J. SAVIGNON: *Communicative Competence: Theory and Classroom Practice. Second Edition.* McGraw-Hill 1997, pages 225, 227

Savignon distinguishes a number of senses of the term 'discrete-point', showing that it can refer to the target of assessment, the mode in which a candidate responds to a task, or the method of evaluating the response. She shows that test tasks can be characterized as a function of these three senses of the term.

Discrete-Point versus Integrative Testing

The word "discrete" means *separate*, or *distinct*, and has been used to describe two different aspects of language tests: (1) content, or *task*, and (2) *mode and scoring of response*. We shall consider each in turn.

A *discrete-point task* is one that focuses on an isolated bit of language, typically surface features of phonology, morphology, syntax, or lexicon... In their purest form, discrete-point items include but one *channel* (oral or written) and one *direction* (receptive or productive); that is, they test "separate" skills of listening, reading, speaking, and writing. In practice, however, this separation is difficult to achieve. A test of speaking may require the prior comprehension of a written or oral "stimulus", a test of listening may include the selection of a correct written response, and so on. Context in discrete-point tasks is usually restricted to a sentence or phrase, but it may also be a longer oral or written text. So long as the criterion remains the recognition or use of a discrete structural feature, this kind of "contextualization", as it is sometimes called, does not alter the basic nature of the task. ...

▷ *Why might it be considered desirable to test skills (reading, speaking, listening, writing) in isolation from one another? On the other hand, why might an integration of skills be thought preferable?*

A *discrete-point* (or objective) *response mode*, in contrast, is a matching, true-false, multiple-choice, or fill-in-the-blank format in which a response is either selected from among alternatives provided or otherwise restricted by the nature of the context provided. This type of response offers ease of scoring and ... high rater reliability. In contrast, a *global response mode* might be an oral interview, a summary of a written or oral text, or a dictation. When a discrete-point mode of response is used, scoring involves the straightforward marking of correct responses. A global response, however, may be evaluated either *discretely*—that is, by looking for and counting distinct linguistic features—or *globally*—that is, by assigning an overall rating based on a combination of features, such as *effectiveness, appropriateness, coherence, comprehensibility, fluency*, and so on. In practice a combination of these scoring methods is often used. Discrete features of pronunciation, spelling, syntax and so forth may be evaluated, while at the same time a general impression of overall quality is established. ... Although test evaluation procedures may vary, in real-life communication it is, of course, always the general impression that prevails.

Generally speaking, the more integrative tasks will require a more global mode of response, whereas a *discrete-point mode of response can be used with both integrative and discrete-point tasks.* The learner's task may be integrative in that it requires inference, or interpretation of meaning, in a text while the response takes the form of a discrete-point selection of the best rejoinder, picture, map, summary, translation, and so on from among alternatives provided.

> In this extract, Savignon is talking about two types of discreteness—what are they?

> Give examples of each of
> – global evaluation of global responses;
> – discrete-point evaluation of global responses;
> – discrete-point evaluation of integrative tasks.

Chapter 4
The rating process

Text 8

T.F. MCNAMARA: *Measuring Second Language Performance*. Longman 1996, pages 123–125

In this extract, a number of ways in which raters differ systematically from one another are discussed.

Let us consider in more detail some of the more important ways in which raters may differ from one another.

1. Two raters may simply differ in their overall leniency.

2. Raters may display particular patterns of harshness or leniency in relation to only one group of candidates, not others, or in relation to particular tasks, not others. That is, there may be an *interaction* involving a rater and some other aspect of the rating situation. Leniency or harshness may not always work in the same direction for all items, or all things being rated. For example, raters in a speaking task may be asked to assess *intelligibility*, *fluency* and *accuracy*; raters may differ from one another in the way they rate any one of these aspects. A rater who overall is fairly lenient may be harsher than other raters when assessing, say, *intelligibility*. It has frequently been found that raters judge aspects of performance to do with control of the formal resources of the language, particularly grammatical structure, more severely than they rate other aspects of the performance … . In general, a rater may be consistently lenient on one item, consistently severe on another; this is a kind of *rater–item* interaction. Or raters may have a tendency to over- or underrate a candidate or class

of candidates; this is an instance of a *rater–candidate* inter-action.

3. Raters may differ from each other in the way they interpret the rating scale they are using. The problem arises because rating scales usually involve discrete rating categories: permissible ratings in the range of 1–6 are quite typical. Imagine a situation where a candidate of given ability falls roughly at the intersection of two of these rating categories; not quite a '3', let us say, but better than most candidates who fall into the category '2'. The rater is forced into an 'either/or' judgment at this point: is the candidate a '3' or not? One rater may consistently score such candidates with a rating of '3', another not. At another point on the ability continuum, the tendency of such judges may be reversed, so that the previously more lenient rater may be harsher at this point on the scale, and vice versa.

We can envisage this in the following way: imagine that candidate ability occupies a continuum. Raters may carve this up in different ways. Compare the way two raters interpret the relationship of the rating scale to this continuum:

1   2   3   4   5   6

1   2   3 4   5   6

Remember that both raters will be working with apparently the same rating scale, graphically displayed as having equal intervals, as follows:

1   2   3   4   5   6

But the appearance of equal intervals here is deceptive; such scales rarely have equal intervals in practice, that is, in the way the available rating categories are interpreted by raters. Moreover, it can be easily shown that raters in their actual interpretation of the scale do not behave in identical ways.

Another way of thinking about these differences between the raters is that, from the point of view of candidates, it will take differing increases in the ability required to have a given chance of achieving a particular score. ...

4. Finally, and rather more obviously, raters may differ in terms of their consistency (or inconsistency); that is, the extent of the random error associated with their ratings. The patterns of scores allocated by a rater may not bear a consistent relationship to those allocated to the same candidates by other raters; sometimes harsher, sometimes more lenient, even allowing for the normal variability in these matters. It makes it hard to say exactly what sort of rater this is, other than that he or she is somewhat erratic; it thus becomes difficult to model the rater's characteristics, and thus to build in some compensation for them. Lack of consistency of this kind is not something that even the most sophisticated technology can do much about, and such raters, once identified, may need to be retrained or, failing this, excluded from the rating process.

▷ *Why do you think raters might judge grammatical features of candidate output more harshly than other features?*

▷ *The text mentions the possibility of an interaction between a rater and a class of candidates. Give examples of situations where this might conceivably arise. What might be done to deal with such situations?*

▷ *What methods might be used to reduce the impact of the tendency of raters to apply different standards in their interpretation of rating scale score categories, or to be internally inconsistent in their interpretation of such categories?*

Text 9
SANDRA J. SAVIGNON: *Communicative Competence: Theory and Classroom Practice.* (2nd edn.) McGraw-Hill 1997, pages 230, 238–9

In this extract, Savignon raises two problems about the use of native speaker competence as a reference point for tests.

Setting Realistic Expectations for L2 Learners
Here we deal with the issue of *realistic expectations for L2 learners* and the *native speaker myth*. It is often assumed that native speakers, or in some cases "educated" native speakers (for example, the FSI Oral Interview), are the model against which L2 learners

are to be evaluated. Native speakers and even educated native speakers, however, differ widely in their communicative competence. ... The most significant difference between the native speaker and the nonnative speaker might well be that the latter is often tested for competence the former is assumed to have. The implications for the construct validity of tests of communicative competence are enormous. Before we can judge the competence of nonnatives we need to better understand the competence of natives. ...

As more valid measures of communicative competence are sought, it seems particularly important that at the very beginning levels (those with which most classroom teachers are concerned) too much emphasis not be assigned to grammatical competence if the standard of accuracy is presumed to be that of an adult "educated native speaker". To expect or even to suggest an expectation of native speaker grammatical accuracy in the spontaneous oral interaction for beginning or even intermediate L2 learners is inauthentic and bound to be a source of frustration for both learners and teachers. Tests designed to "test the subjunctive", or other such linguistic elements, are at this beginning level best confined to discrete-point modes of response whereby learners are given ample time to monitor their response and focus on form rather than on meaning. This recommendation should not be interpreted to mean that grammar is unimportant. At issue, rather, is the appropriateness of adult native-speaker standards for beginners. Descriptions of oral proficiency at all levels, moreover, should be stated in terms of what learners can do in a functional sense rather than in terms of the structural features they have not yet mastered.

▷ *Think of examples of performance on communicative tasks in which it cannot be assumed that native speakers will have an intrinsic advantage over non-native speakers.*

▷ *In what areas other than grammar might it be sensible to make concessions in our expectations of the performance of learners who are in the early stages of learning?*

Text 10

D.E. INGRAM and ELAINE WYLIE: 'Assessing speaking proficiency in the International English Language Testing System' in Dan Douglas and Carol Chapelle (eds.): *A New Decade of Language Testing Research: Selected Papers from the 1990 Language Testing Research Colloquium*. Teachers of English to Speakers of Other Languages 1993, page 224

The authors of this extract provide an example of the kinds of operational constraints which force compromises in the conduct of testing procedures. The context in which they are writing is the revision of the British Council's English Language Testing Service (ELTS). This test was used to screen the English language abilities of prospective international students wishing to study in the U.K. The revision process led to the introduction of the IELTS test (see Chapter 1).

An interview was used to test speaking in the former ELTS and, despite some concerns about reliability, the ELTS Revision Steering Committee felt that this feature of the test should be retained. However, the committee was faced with financial and other operational constraints very similar to those that had ruled out the possibility of any direct assessment of speaking in the TOEFL.... In order to constrain administration costs, it was decided that the interview should last no longer than 15 minutes (and no less than 11 minutes) out of a total length for the IELTS test of 145 minutes. Cost factors also excluded the possibility of involving a second person for interview, a technique that [it had been found] gave greater reliability and that is used for all interviews for the U.S. government.... The other major constraining factor is that the test has to be administrable anywhere in the world, often in circumstances in which relatively little control can be exercised over the selection and skills of interviewers. To maximize reliability, therefore, the interview has been tightly structured to control what the interviewer can do, and a process of monitoring of interview quality and rating accuracy is built into administrative proceedings.

▷ *What measures might be taken to monitor interview quality and rating accuracy? What risk to fairness might remain from involving only a single person in the interview?*

Text 11

SARA CUSHING WEIGLE: 'Using FACETS to model rater
training effects' in *Language Testing* 15, 1998, pages 263–4

*Testing is all about compromise, and a frequent source of
compromise is a conflict between our understanding of what
it is desirable to include in the assessment procedure and our
practical ability to do so. Here the issue arises not in relation
to the performance of candidates but the behaviour of raters.*

It is generally accepted among specialists in both writing assessment and educational measurement that rater training is essential
in achieving reliable ratings of essay examinations. However, in
both the writing-assessment and measurement literature some
controversy exists as to the purpose and efficacy of rater training.
In the writing-assessment literature, concerns have been voiced
about the validity of holistic essay-examination scores because of
the artificiality of the procedures used to reach acceptable rater
reliability, including training…. It has been argued that an
emphasis on rater consensus may force raters to ignore their own
experience and expertise in judging writing, which are viewed as
essential components of the interactive reading process…, and
that inter-rater agreement may only be possible when raters are
agreeing on superficial aspects of the text….

On the other hand, essay scoring and rater-training procedures
are presumably founded on the premise that an essay examination is measuring a particular ability which can be defined operationally and measured accurately if raters can be trained to agree
on the definition of the ability. From this point of view, it is essential for raters to put aside their own subjective experience in order
to adopt the agreed-upon scoring criteria for the examination.
Thus a tension exists in the writing-assessment literature between
these two viewpoints on the function of rater training in writing
assessment.

▷ *Why might the experience and expertise of raters be seen as
essential components of the interactive reading process
involved in the rating of writing? What practical dilemmas
does this create for assessment?*

▷ *Weigle presents a case where the demands of testing on the one hand, in this case the need to constrain the rating process, and an understanding of the test construct on the other, are at odds. What other examples can you think of where it is impossible to include in a test or testing procedure something we feel it is important to include? (Consider the discussion of this issue as it relates to test content in Chapter 3).*

Chapter 5
Validity: Testing the test

Text 12
LYLE F. BACHMAN and ADRIAN S. PALMER: *Language Testing in Practice: Designing and Developing Useful Language Tests.* Oxford University Press 1996, page 21

Bachman and Palmer draw on the validity theory of the great educational assessment thinker Samuel Messick in their discussions of construct validity. Bachman and Palmer have examined the implications of Messick's work for language testing in a series of landmark papers and texts. Their approach focuses on an understanding of the nature of communicative language ability underlying test performance, and the relationship between test design and the contexts of future test use, which they define as the Target Language Use (TLU) domain or situation.

Construct validity pertains to the meaningfulness and appropriateness of the *interpretations* that we make on the basis of test scores. When we interpret scores from language tests as indicators of test takers' language ability, a crucial question is, 'To what extent can we justify these interpretations?' The clear implication of this question is that as test developers and test users we must be able to provide adequate justification for any interpretation we make of a given test score. That is, we need to demonstrate, or justify, the validity of the interpretations we make of test scores, and not simply assert or argue that they are valid.

In order to justify a particular score interpretation, we need to provide evidence that the test score reflects the area(s) of language ability we want to measure, and very little else. In order to provide such evidence, we must define the construct that we want to measure. For our purposes, we can consider a construct to be the specific definition of an ability that provides the basis for a given test or test task and for interpreting scores derived from this task. The term construct validity is therefore used to refer to the extent to which we can interpret a test score as an indicator of the ability(ies), or construct(s), we want to measure. Construct validity also has to do with the domain of generalization to which our score interpretations generalize. The domain of generalization is the set of tasks in the T[arget] L[anguage] U[se] domain to which the test tasks correspond. At the very least we want our interpretations about language ability to generalize beyond the testing situation itself to a particular TLU domain.

▷ *Bachman and Palmer speak of interpretations of test scores. What do they mean by this? Give one or more examples.*

▷ *Construct validity according to Bachman and Palmer involves two types of generalization from test performances. How does this compare with the discussion of the relationship of test and criterion in Chapter 1?*

Text 13

ALAN DAVIES: 'The role of the segmental dictionary in professional validation: Constructing a dictionary of language testing' in Alister Cumming and Richard Berwick (eds): *Validation in Language Testing*. Multilingual Matters 1996, pages 233–234

Language testing can be a technical field involving a considerable amount of precise and specialized vocabulary. Alan Davies and his colleagues in Melbourne have produced the first dictionary of language testing, to help educators and researchers who need to understand literature in the field. Here is a near final draft of one of the entries.

FACE VALIDITY
A type of VALIDITY referring to the degree to which a test appears to measure the knowledge or abilities it claims to measure, as judged by an untrained observer (such as the candidate taking the test, or the institution which plans to administer it).

For example, a gate-keeping test administered prior to entry to a particular profession (e.g. dentistry) which simulates actual work-place conditions can be said to have high face validity (even though the skills measured may not in fact be reliable predictors of future performance).

Conversely, if a test of listening comprehension uses a speaker with a strong regional accent which is unfamiliar to the majority of the candidates, the test may be judged as lacking face validity. A more obvious example of poor face validity is the use of a dictation activity to measure an apparently unrelated skills such as speaking ability (although there may be empirical evidence of a high correlation between the two skills).

The term is often used in a pejorative senses ...

However, [some authors] argue that failure to take issues of face validity into account may jeopardize the public credibility of a test (and indeed the curriculum on which the test may be based) and that the notion of 'test appeal' insofar as it is achievable is a practical consideration which test designers cannot afford to overlook. DIRECT TESTS are in fact often produced out of a concern for face validity.

See also CONTENT VALIDITY (a clear distinction is not always made between the two terms).

▷ *Why might the term face validity be used in a pejorative sense? How important is it for a test to have face validity?*

▷ *Explain the remark about the connection between direct tests and face validity.*

▷ *How might face validity and content validity be connected in such a way that they are not always clearly distinguished?*

Text 14

LYLE F. BACHMAN: *Fundamental Considerations in Language Testing.* Oxford University Press 1990, pages 72–76

In an extract from his classic text, Lyle Bachman discusses norm-referenced measurement (the basis for the psychometric-structuralist approach to testing (see Text 2) associated with Lado (see Text 3)), and contrasts it with criterion-referenced measurement, an approach more com-patible with communicative tests.

Norm-referenced tests

Norm-referenced (NR) tests are designed to enable the test user to make 'normative' interpretations of test results. That is, test results are interpreted with reference to the performance of a given group, or norm. The 'norm group' is typically a large group of individuals who are similar to the individuals for whom the test is designed. In the development of NR tests the norm group is given the test, and then the characteristics, or norms, of this group's performance are used as reference points for interpreting the performance of other students who take the test. The perfor-mance characteristics, or norms, most typically used as reference points are the mean $\bar{x}$, or average score of the group, and the standard deviation s, which is an indicator of how spread out the scores of the group are. ...

In order to provide the most easily interpretable results, NR tests are designed to maximize the distinctions among the individ-uals in a given group. Such tests are also sometimes referred to as 'psychometric' tests since most theoretical models of psychomet-rics, or psychological measurement, are based on the assumption of a normal distribution and maximizing the variations among individuals' scores.

Criterion-referenced tests

Criterion-referenced (CR) tests are designed to enable the test user to interpret a test score with reference to a criterion level of ability or domain of content. An example would be the case in which stu-dents are evaluated in terms of their relative degree of mastery of course content, rather than with respect to their relative ranking in the class. Thus, all students who master the course content might receive an 'A', irrespective of how many students achieve this grade. The primary concerns in developing a CR test are that it adequately represent the criterion ability level or sample the con-tent domain, and that it be sensitive to levels of ability or degrees of mastery of the different components of that domain. ...

The two primary distinctions between NR and CR tests are (1) in their design, construction, and development; and (2) in the scales they yield and the interpretation of these scales. NR tests are designed and developed to maximize distinctions among individual test takers, which means that the items or parts of such tests will be selected according to how well they discriminate individuals who do well on the test as a whole from those who do poorly. CR tests, on the other hand, are designed to be representative of specified levels of ability or domains of content, and the items or parts will be selected according to how adequately they represent these ability levels or content domains. And while NR scores are interpreted with reference to the performance of other individuals on the test, CR test scores are interpreted as indicators of a level of ability or degree of mastery of the content domain. . . .

Despite these differences, however, it is important to understand that these two frames of reference are not necessarily mutually exclusive.

▷ *How might norm-referenced and criterion-referenced tests differ in their design?*

▷ *Given the differences between the two types of test, how is it that they are 'not mutually exclusive', according to Bachman?*

Text 15

ROSEMARY BAKER: *Classical Test Theory and Item Response Theory in Test Analysis. Special Report 2: Language Testing Update.* Centre for Research in Language Education 1997, pages 19–20

Item Response Theory (IRT) often seems a dauntingly technical field, and various attempts have been made to mediate it for readers who are untrained in measurement theory. This is certainly necessary within language testing, where most readers of the literature will be unlikely to have much background in psychometrics or statistics. Baker's is one of the first such attempts; it was written as part of a PhD thesis in 1987.

Item Response Theory
The rest of this chapter is concerned with the approach to test theory variously known as 'latent trait (LT) theory', 'item characteristic curve (ICC) theory', 'Item Response Theory' (IRT), and, occasionally, as 'modern test theory'. . . .

The first of these terms recalls the origins of this approach in psychology, where ... 'latent trait' denotes a psychological dimension necessary for the psychological description of individuals, i.e. a hypothetical construct ... which is assumed to underlie observed behaviour.... In the context of testing, latent traits are conceived of as characteristics or attributes which account for consistencies in the individual's responses to items ....

... The term 'latent traits' has sometimes been taken to refer to fixed, unchanging, causal entities; however, ... latent traits should not be thought of as fixed, since a trait such as 'achievement' is capable of change or improvement, e.g. as a result of instruction. ... A trait orientation to psychological theory carries no necessary implication that traits exist in any physical or physiological sense. These comments apply equally to the notion of latent trait as it is used in the measurement context.

The term 'item characteristic curve theory' ... derives from one of the concepts central to this approach, while 'modern test theory' emphasises the departure from the classical approach. The term 'Item Response Theory' ... appears generally to be gaining currency.

Central Concepts in IRT
The central feature of an IRT approach is that a relationship is specified between observable performance on test items and the unobservable characteristics or abilities assumed to underlie this performance .... The characteristic measured by a given set of items, whether a psychological attribute, a skill, or some aspect of educational achievement, is conceived of as an underlying continuum, often referred to as a latent trait or latent variable. ...

This underlying continuum is represented by a numerical scale, upon which a person's standing can be estimated using his/her responses to suitable test items. Items measuring the trait are seen as being located on the same scale, according to the trait level required of testees.

Person Ability and Item Difficulty
A person's standing on the scale is frequently called his/her 'ability'. As the use of this term is a potential source of misunderstanding, it must be emphasised that it refers to whatever

characteristic, skill or area of understanding the test measures. ...
The term 'ability' is used simply to mean the typical or expected
performance of an individual in the area represented by the class
of test questions.

An item's location on the scale is usually called its 'difficulty',
particularly in the case of educational tests ... . (Clearly, the concept of item difficulty is less applicable to the measurement of attitudes or personality traits, and location on the scale in this
context is more appropriately thought of as the trait level embodied in the item.)

Central to IRT, therefore, is the notion that persons can be
placed on a scale on the basis of their ability in a given area, and
that items measuring this ability can be placed on the same scale.
Thus there is "... a single scale ... which measures (is) both difficulty and ability simultaneously" (Alastair Pollitt, 1979, page
58). It is via this scale that the connection between items and
respondents, ... the essence of IRT, can be made.

▷ *What is implied by the use of the terms 'latent' or 'underlying'
to describe the ability measured in tests of this type? How does
this relate to the issues raised in Chapter 1 on the relationship
between test and criterion?*

▷ *What problems does Baker raise in relation to the use of the
terms 'ability' and 'difficulty' in IRT? Do these same issues
appear to arise in relation to the use of these terms in other test
theories?*

Text 16
SAMUEL MESSICK: 'Validity and washback in language
testing' in *Language Testing* 13, 1996, pages 251–253

*In this extract, Messick discusses the notion of consequential
validity in the context of concerns for the washback of tests.
He relates his discussion to two aspects of validity introduced
in Chapter 5: 'construct under-representation' and 'construct-
irrelevant variance'.*

The *consequential* aspect of construct validity includes evidence
and rationales for evaluating the intended and unintended consequences of score interpretation and use in both the short- and

long-term, especially those associated with bias in scoring and interpretation, with unfairness in test use, and with positive or negative washback effects on teaching and learning. However, this form of evidence should not be viewed in isolation as a separate type of validity, say, of 'consequential validity' or, worse still, 'washback validity'. Rather, because the social values served in the intended and unintended outcomes of test interpretation and use both derive from and contribute to the meaning of test scores, appraisal of social consequences of the testing is also seen to be subsumed as an aspect of construct validity... .

Consequences associated with testing are likely to be a function of numerous factors in the context or setting and in the persons responding as well as in the content and form of the test. ...

The primary measurement concern with respect to adverse consequences is that negative washback, or, indeed, any negative impact on individuals or groups should not derive from any source of test invalidity such as construct under-representation or construct-irrelevant variance ... . That is, invalidly low scores should not occur because the assessment is missing something relevant to the focal construct that, if present, would have permitted the affected person to display their competence. Moreover, invalidly low scores should not occur because the measurement contains something irrelevant that interferes with the affected persons' demonstration of competence.

Furthermore, if what is under-represented in the assessment of communicative competence is an important part of the criterion performance, such as listening and speaking as opposed to reading and writing, then invalidly high scores may be attained by examinees well prepared on the represented skills but ill prepared on the under-represented ones. That is, scores may be invalidly high as indicators of communicative competence even though they are valid measures of reading and writing proficiency. Invalidly high scores may also be obtained by testwise examinees who are facile in dealing with construct-irrelevant difficulty. ...

If important constructs or aspects of constructs are under-represented on the test, teachers might come to overemphasize those constructs that are well represented and downplay those that are not. If the test employs unfamiliar item formats or stresses knowledge of grammar, for instance, to the detriment of communicative competence, teachers might pay undue attention to overcoming the irrelevant difficulty as opposed to fostering communicative proficiency. One defence against such adverse consequences is to provide test familiarization and preparation materials to reduce the effects of construct-irrelevant difficulty and attendant test anxiety, but the best defence is to minimize such irrelevant difficulty in the first place as well as construct under-representation.

In contrast, adverse consequences associated with the valid measurement of current status—such as validly low scores resulting from poor teaching or limited opportunity to learn—are not the test makers' responsibility. Such adverse consequences of valid assessment represent problems not of measurement, but rather of teaching and of educational and social policy.

▷ *Give examples of the way in which each of these factors might be associated with the consequences of testing: the test context; the testees; the test content; the format of the test.*

▷ *What limits does Messick see to the social responsibility of the language tester?*

Text 17

DIANNE WALL and J. CHARLES ALDERSON: 'Examining washback: The Sri Lankan impact study' in Alister Cumming and Richard Berwick (eds.): *Validation in Language Testing.* Multilingual Matters 1996, pages 200–1, 219–220

The authors of this extract were led to revise their theory of washback on the basis of the findings of a study of the impact on teaching and learning of a new communicative syllabus for EFL in Sri Lankan secondary schools.

The Washback Hypothesis ... implies that a test on its own makes all the difference. If it is a 'good' test (i.e. it reflects the aims of the syllabus, and its content and method) then it will produce positive washback; if it is a 'bad' test (if it does not) then it will produce negative washback.

Alderson and Wall (1993) discuss possible refinements to the basic Washback Hypothesis by distinguishing content of teaching from the methodology used, and teaching from learning, as well as addressing the need to consider the impact of a test not only on teaching and learning but also on attitudes, material and effort. We were to come to understand, through our attempts to establish washback and understand its nature, that what is not mentioned in any of the formulations of the Washback Hypothesis are the other factors that might also contribute to what teaching will look like: Do the teachers understand the approach of the textbook? Are they prepared to accept this? Are they able to implement the new ideas? Are they aware of the nature of the exam? Are they willing to go along with its demands? Are they able to prepare their students for what is to come? We return to these important points in the concluding section of this chapter. ...

We now believe that an exam on its own cannot reinforce an approach to teaching that the educational system has not adequately prepared its teachers for. Factors which may prevent the implementation of the new approach, and which may make the task of reinforcement by an examination (washback) difficult include frequent turnover in teaching staff, lack of material resources, management practices within schools, insufficient exam-specific teacher training, inadequate communication between those responsible for the exam and its users, inadequate understanding of the philosophy of the textbook or the examination, teachers' beliefs that a particular method is more effective than those represented by the textbook or implicit in the examination, the degree of commitment of teachers to the profession, other obligations, including teaching commitments in their institutions or privately, and so on. ...

In short, if an exam is to have the impact intended, educationalists and education managers need to consider a range of factors that affect how innovations succeed or fail and that influence teacher (and pupil) behaviours. The exam is only one of these factors. . . .

On the basis of our results, we believe the Washback Hypothesis to be overly simplistic and in need of considerable further discussion, refinement and investigation. We have produced convincing evidence, in the Sri Lankan context, that tests have an impact on *what* teachers teach but not on *how* they teach. We have explored some of the factors that contribute to and inhibit washback, and have implied, at least, that the nature of curricular innovations is much more complex than the advocates or critics of washback seem to understand. Testers need to pay much more attention to the washback of their tests, but they should also guard against oversimplified beliefs that 'good' tests will automatically have 'good' impact. Washback needs to be studied and understood, not asserted.

▷ *Why should a test maker be cautious in thinking that a good test will have positive washback?*

▷ *Wall and Alderson seems to be acknowledging the limits to the power of the language test and the language tester. How does this compare with the view of tests and the responsibility of test makers taken by advocates of Critical Language Testing (see pages 76–7, and Text 19 below)?*

Text 18

BERNARD SPOLSKY: *Measured Words.* Oxford University Press 1995, pages 15–16

Spolsky sketches the influence of the writings of the French theorist Michel Foucault in the development of critical perspectives on the social and political role and power of tests

Social or political purposes lend tests and examinations their critical weight, as Michel Foucault indicated in a book he entitled *Surveiller et punir: naissance de la prison.* The first section of this book deals with torture, the second with punishment, and the third with discipline, and it is here that examinations are discussed. Examinations, Foucault explained, provide 'a normalizing gaze, a surveillance that makes it possible to qualify, to classify and to punish' (Foucault: 1975: 186–7). He proposed an analogy to the way that doctors developed authority over hospitals. Before the seventeenth century the hospital was essentially dominated by the nursing and administrative staff, with only occasional visits by doctors. The innovation of a series of regular daily examinations by physicians gave doctors pre-eminent power over the establishment, and changed the hospital into 'a place of training and of the correlations of knowledge' (ibid.: 188). In the same way, the institution of regular examinations in the eighteenth century transformed the school into 'a sort of apparatus of uninterrupted examination' (ibid.). As a result of examinations, knowledge started to flow not just from teacher to pupil, but back from pupil to teacher, establishing a science of education, in much the same way that information flowing from examined patients to their doctors had instituted a 'discipline' of medicine.

The examination, Foucault suggested, was a mechanism linking power and knowledge. It was a ritualized ceremony that required the subjects to be seen, and transformed them into objects under control. It built an archive of documentation: the markbook of the teacher, the papers and scores of the candidates became 'a whole meticulous archive' (ibid.: 191) in which the population of the school could be ordered and fixed for ever in its place, and it transformed the individual into 'a case' preserved as an object.

▷ *If tests function in society in the way that Foucault suggests, can this function be altered by making language testing practice more ethical or more valid?*

Text 19

ELANA SHOHAMY: 'Critical Language Testing and Beyond', in *Studies in Education* 24, 1998, pages 331–345

In her seminal paper on Critical Language Testing, Elana Shohamy sets out a programme of issues facing test developers, teachers and testing researchers which are raised from this perspective.

Critical language testing claims that the act of language testing is not neutral. Rather, it is a product and agent of cultural, social, political, educational and ideological agendas that shape the lives of individual participants, teachers and learners.

- Critical Language Testing views test takers as political subjects in a political context.
- It views language tests as tools directly related to levels of success, deeply embedded, in cultural, educational and political arenas where different ideological and social forms are in struggle.
- It asks questions about what sort of agendas are delivered through tests and whose agendas they are.

- It challenges psychometric traditions and considers interpretive ones.
- It claims that language testers need to ask themselves what sort of vision of society language tests create and what vision of society tests are used for; are language tests merely intended to fulfill predefined curricular or proficiency goals or do they have other agendas.
- It asks questions about whose knowledge the tests are based on; is what is included on language tests "truth" to be handed on to test takers, or is it something that can be negotiated, challenged and appropriated?
- It considers the meaning of language test scores, and the degree to which they are prescriptive, final, absolute, and the extent to which they are open to discussion and interpretations.
- It perceives language testing as being caught up in an array of questions concerning educational and social systems; the notion of 'just a test' is an impossibility because it is impossible to separate language testing from the many contexts in which it operates.

Critical language testing signifies a paradigm shift in language testing in that it introduces new criteria for the validity of language tests. Consequential, systemic, interpretive and ethical are a few of the new forms of validity, calling for the need to collect empirical data on language tests' use. Such evidence may show that tests considered valid in the past, may not be so if they are shown to have negative consequences.

▷ *In Text 14, Bachman refers to norm-referenced tests as 'psychometric' tests. Shohamy speaks of critical language testing as challenging psychometric traditions. Why might norm-referenced tests be the particular target of challenge by advocates of critical language testing?*

▷ *What similarities and differences are there between the position advocated by Shohamy here and that taken by Messick in Text 16?*

Text 20
HAROLD S. MADSEN: 'Computer-adaptive testing of listening and reading comprehension' in Patricia Dunkel

(ed.): *Computer-Assisted Language Learning and Testing: Research Issues and Practice.* Newbury House 1991, pages 238–241

Madsen distinguishes a number of ways in which the computer can be involved in language test delivery or scoring or both. He considers the advantages and drawbacks of computerized language testing to date.

One computer-based language testing option is to allow for human interaction in the evaluation process. Of the various computer-assisted testing (CAT) procedures involving live examiner participation, the test essay is a classic example. It utilizes the computer as a word processor… , allowing the writer to tap such computer resources as a dictionary and thesaurus. … The bulk of the essay evaluation is conducted by human critiquers. This approach allows for maximum creativity and communicative expression on the part of the candidate, while making allowance for the still rather primitive state of the art as far as productive language skill correction via computer is concerned.

A second computer-assisted test (or CAT) option has been labeled in Britain as CBELT—computer-based English language testing…. This approach uses any of a wide variety of procedures in test delivery. But unlike the previous option, CBELT is scored exclusively by computer. This constraint tends to restrict somewhat the scope of item types that can be successfully administered. … Rapid, accurate correction of the test could be provided for such items as multiple-choice reading comprehension questions, objective lexical and grammatical questions, editing procedures, and even some translation tasks.

On the surface, the computer-adaptive language test (CALT) resembles the CBELT version of CAT: it is computer-driven and computer-scored. But unlike CBELT, the adaptive test is uniquely tailored for each student…. The adaptive or "tailored' computer test accesses a specially calibrated item bank and is driven by a statistical routine which analyzes student responses to questions and selects items for the candidate that are of appropriate difficulty. Then, when a specified standard error of measurement level has been reached, the exam is terminated. In short, the format of CALT often resembles that utilized in CAT. The essential difference is the psychometrically sound tailoring process in computer-adaptive tests, which provides for a more effective measure of language proficiency.

Limitations and Advantages of Computer Testing
The potential limitations of computerized language testing are serious enough to warrant the careful attention of those planning to use this medium. A recurring concern is the high cost of computer hardware and software. Other misgivings include the time required to acquaint examinees with the computer, the potential of double jeopardy (inadvertently evaluating not only language but also computer expertise), and the potential of subjecting test candidates to debilitating levels of anxiety as result of the need to manipulate the new technology. Related to these concerns is the matter of potential bias in computerized exams against those unfamiliar with the new technology.... Of course with the increase in computer literacy and the increasing availability of computers in schools and other organizations, some of these objections begin to diminish. ...

A final and very serious limitation, one characteristic of both computer-assisted and adaptive tests, is the tendency to utilize, almost exclusively, objectively scored language exams. The result appears to be a neglect of sound testing procedures using the essay, dictation, and oral interview. ...

Despite the concerns and limitations enumerated above, there are of course compelling advantages offered by computerized tests in general, and adaptive tests in particular. ...

The advantages of computer-assisted or -adaptive testing include the following: the convenience of providing exam results immediately (this convenience results in savings in teacher-secretarial effort and is a boon to students); the benefit of accurate, consistent evaluation; diagnostic assistance to teachers and administrators; relief to test writers (as far as rapid editing and revision of test items is concerned); and swift access to banks of test items. Test types other than multiple-choice questions can also be administered (e.g., the cloze which requires words to be typed into blanks in a prose passage); scaled items (e.g., examiner ratings of student responses that range from 0 to 4 on an oral interview); and even essay exams, which are scored later by the teacher examiner. Furthermore, the tedious problem of deciphering student handwriting is eliminated.

The special advantages of computer-adaptive tests ... can be summarized here. Experimental findings reveal their superiority to paper-and-pencil tests in terms of reliability and validity, particularly when relatively few items are administered .... Research has shown the excellent predictive power of combined CALT and non-CALT measurement ..., thus encouraging the use not only of objective measures but also of sound procedures not amenable at the present time to tailored computer testing. CALT likewise provides for ... items tailored to the ability level of the examinee, virtual elimination of cheating during the exam, flexibility in scheduling tests since each administration is a unique exam, successful use of small item pools..., test linking and networking, and greatly improved test efficiency, including a substantial reduction in time for each exam....

▷ Explain the essential differences between the terms 'computer-assisted testing', 'computer-based language testing' and 'computer-adaptive language testing'.

▷ In what contexts might the advantages of computer-adaptive language tests be particularly relevant, and in what contexts might they be less compelling?

▷ What issues might be raised in a discussion of the way in which language tests are coming to rely on the use of computer technology? (see Chapter 7 and Text 19)

SECTION 3
References

The references which follow can be classified into introductory level (marked ■□□), more advanced, and consequently more technical (marked ■■□), and specialized, very demanding (marked ■■■).

Chapter 1
Testing, testing ... What is a language test?

■■□

LYLE F. BACHMAN and ADRIAN S. PALMER: *Language Testing in Practice: Designing and Developing Useful Language Tests*. Oxford University Press 1996 (*see* Text 12)

A thorough introduction to language testing theory and practice, based around the influential theoretical position of the authors on the nature and measurement of communicative language ability.

■■□

CAROLINE M. CLAPHAM and DAVID CORSON (eds.): *Language Testing and Assessment*, Volume 7 of *Encyclopaedia of Language and Education*. Kluwer Academic 1997

This volume provides valuable overviews of research in most areas of language testing.

■☐☐

JOHN L. D. CLARK and RAY T. CLIFFORD: 'The FSI/ILR/ACTFL proficiency scales and testing techniques: Development, current status and needed research' in *Studies in Second Language Acquisition* 10/2, 1988

This paper outlines the history of the development of the Oral Proficiency Interview (OPI), discusses its approach to assessment, and presents the scales used in rating performances.

■☐☐

ALAN DAVIES *et al.*: *Mark My Words* [video programmes]. Language Testing Research Centre, University of Melbourne 1996

A series of six 20-minute professionally produced video programmes, presenting in a lively and accessible fashion basic concepts and procedures in language testing.

■■☐

ALAN DAVIES *et al.*: *Dictionary of Language Testing*. Cambridge University Press 1999

A sourcebook of comprehensive explanations of terms and procedures in language testing.

Chapter 2
Communication and the design of language tests

■■☐

LYLE F. BACHMAN: *Fundamental Considerations in Language Testing*. Oxford University Press 1990 (*see* Texts 6 and 14)

This classic text provides the most authoritative discussion to date of a range of fundamental issues in language testing. It is perhaps best known for Bachman's model of communicative language ability.

■■■

MICHAEL CANALE and MERRILL SWAIN: 'Theoretical
bases of communicative approaches to second language
teaching and testing' in *Applied Linguistics* 1/1, 1980
(*see* Text 5)

Much-cited discussion of the implications of Hymes's theory of
communicative competence for language testing.

■□□

J. B. CARROLL: 'Fundamental considerations in testing for
English language proficiency of foreign students' in Center
for Applied Linguistics: *Testing the English Proficiency of
Foreign Students*. Center for Applied Linguistics 1961
Reprinted in H.B. Allen and R.N. Campbell (eds.): *Teaching
English as a Second Language: A Book of Readings*.
McGraw-Hill 1972

Though not primarily a language tester, Carroll, in this much-
cited paper, anticipated the development of communicative language tests, including tests of language for specific purposes such
as those used in the selection of international students.

■□□

ROBERT LADO: *Language Testing: The Construction and
Use of Foreign Language Tests*. Longman 1961 (*see* Text 2)

This classic text influenced a generation of language teachers and
test designers in its rigorous view of the necessary constraints on
the testability of second language proficiency.

■■□

KEITH MORROW: 'Communicative language testing:
revolution or evolution?' in C.J. Brumfit and K. Johnson
(eds.) *The Communicative Approach to Language Teaching*.
Oxford University Press 1979

This paper discusses communicative language tests as performance tests, and proposes an influential list of presumed reading
microskills as the basis for the construction of communicative
tests of reading.

■■□

JOHN OLLER: *Language Tests at School*. Longman 1979

This was the most important book on language testing of its period. It proposed a category of integrative tests that foreshadowed the introduction of communicative language tests and popularized the cloze test in language testing.

■■■

JOHN OLLER (ed.): *Issues in Language Testing Research*. Newbury House 1983

The collection of papers in this book illustrates the debate about the types of integrative test proposed by Oller, and the successful critique of his claims about the merits of cloze tests.

■■□

BERNARD SPOLSKY: 'Introduction: Linguists and language testers' in B. Spolsky (ed.): *Approaches to Language Testing. [Advances in Language Testing Series: 2]* Center for Applied Linguistics 1978

This influential paper contains a discussion of the recent history of language testing in terms of three distinct periods of theory and practice.

Chapter 3
The testing cycle

■□□

GEOFF BRINDLEY: *Assessing Achievement in the Learner Centred Curriculum*. National Centre for English Language Teaching and Research 1989

Originally written for teachers of English to adult immigrants in Australia, this remains one of the two or three best books available to date on methods of communicative language assessment for classroom teachers.

■■□

BRIAN K. LYNCH and FRED G. DAVIDSON: 'Criterion-referenced language test development: linking curricula, teachers, and tests' in *TESOL Quarterly* 28/4, 1994

This paper shows teachers how to design criterion-referenced tests (see Chapter 6) through an iterative process of designing and revising test specifications and related test materials.

■□□

ELANA SHOHAMY: *A Practical Handbook in Language Testing for the Second Language Teacher*. Tel Aviv University 1985

This book, originally written for students in the author's own programme, achieved widespread circulation because of its extremely accessible and practical advice for teachers on the design and construction of language tests.

■□□

BERNARD SPOLSKY: 'The limits of authenticity in language testing' in *Language Testing* 2/1, 1985

This is a helpful theoretical and practical discussion of the necessary constraints on authenticity in communicative language tests. The issue of *Language Testing* in which the paper appears is devoted to the topic of authenticity in language tests and contains a number of other valuable papers.

■□□

CYRIL J. WEIR: *Communicative Language Testing*. Prentice Hall 1990
CYRIL J. WEIR: *Understanding and Developing Language Tests*. Prentice Hall 1993

These two handbooks of test design and construction for language teachers offer practical advice on a range of topics and procedures.

Chapter 4
The rating process

■■□

J. CHARLES ALDERSON: 'Bands and scores' in J. Charles Alderson and B. North (eds.): *Language Testing in the 1990s*. Modern English Publications and The British Council 1991

This paper offers a helpful account of the different purposes of rating scales and the implications for their construction and wording.

■■■

ANNE BROWN: 'The effect of rater variables in the development of an occupation-specific language performance test' in *Language Testing* 12/1, 1995

This paper constitutes an example of research into the complexities of performance assessment of spoken language, in this case by looking at the influence of rater backgrounds on assessments in an advanced test of Japanese for tour guides.

Chapter 5
Validity: testing the test

■■□

ALAN DAVIES: 'Validating three tests of English language proficiency' in *Language Testing* 1/1, 1984

This paper offers an account of the writer's experience of developing proficiency tests including specific purpose communicative tests, and illustrates the British emphasis on content validity in performance tests.

■■□

A. HUGHES, D. PORTER and C. J. WEIR (eds.): *ELTS Validation Project: Proceedings of a Conference Held to Consider the ELTS Validation Project Report*. ('English Language Testing Service Research Report 1 (ii)'). British Council/University of Cambridge Local Examinations Certificate 1988

The papers in this volume collectively provide an example of the discussion of principle and the interpretation of empirical evidence that together form the process of test validation, in this case in the context of the development of the IELTS test.

■■■

SAMUEL MESSICK: 'Validity' in R.L. Linn (ed.):
Educational measurement. (3rd edn.) Macmillan 1989

This authoritative discussion of validity constituted a revolution in thinking on the subject, among other things for its introduction of the notion of consequential validity (*see* Text 16).

■■■

SAMUEL MESSICK: 'The interplay of evidence and consequences in the validation of performance assessments' in
Educational Researcher 23/2, 1994.

This is a shorter, more accessible introduction to Messick's validity theory and is particularly useful for its discussion of issues relevant to the design of communicative language tests.

Chapter 6
Measurement

■■■

ROSEMARY BAKER: *Classical Test Theory and Item Response Theory in Test Analysis.* Special Report 2:
Language Testing Update. Centre for Research in Language Education 1997 (*see* Text 15)

This discussion of Item Response Theory, particularly Rasch analysis, originally part of the author's PhD dissertation, was one of the first written for a language testing readership.

■■□

GRANT HENNING: *A Guide to Language Testing:
Development, Evaluation, Research.* Newbury House 1987

This is a useful guide to many of the technical aspects of language test design and construction, and provides accessible introductions to a number of important standard psychometric procedures.

■■■

T. F. MCNAMARA: *Measuring Second Language Performance*. Longman 1996

This book provides a detailed but non-technical introduction to Rasch measurement and explores its application in research on second language performance assessment. In the early chapters, the book offers a critique of the models of Canale and Swain (*see* Text 5) and Bachman in the context of a careful discussion of the notion of 'performance' in second languages.

■□□

ALASTAIR POLLITT: 'Giving students a sporting chance: Assessment by counting and judging' in J. Charles Alderson and B. North (eds.): *Language Testing in the 1990s*. Modern English Publications and The British Council 1991

The author provides a lively non-specialist conceptual introduction to contrasting approaches to measurement.

Chapter 7
The social character of language tests

■■□

J. CHARLES ALDERSON and DIANNE WALL (eds.): *Language Testing* 13/3 (Special Issue on washback), 1996

This collection of papers addresses washback from a variety of viewpoints, and includes an important paper by Samuel Messick clarifying the relationship between washback and consequential validity (*see* Texts 16 and 17).

■■□

GEOFF BRINDLEY: 'Outcomes-based assessment and reporting in language learning programs: A review of the issues' in *Language Testing* 15/1, 1998

Brindley provides the clearest overview to date of the trend towards scale and framework based assessment in school and vocational education contexts in a number of settings internationally.

■■☐

A. DAVIES (ed.): *Language Testing* 14/3 (Special Issue on ethics in language testing), 1997

These papers present different positions on the ethical responsibility of language testers, and discuss practical language testing contexts in which ethical issues arise.

■☐☐

F. ALLAN HANSON: *Testing Testing: Social Consequences of the Examined Life*. University of California Press 1993

This very readable book provides an introduction to the way in which all testing can be seen as a social practice, thus involving a range of political and ethical considerations.

■■☐

M. B. KANE and R. MITCHELL (eds.): *Implementing Performance Assessment: Promises, Problems and Challenges*. Lawrence Erlbaum 1996

While not in the area of language testing, this collection of papers provides an excellent overview of the rationale for performance assessment in school settings. It provides a particularly clear contextualization for much of the discussion of ethics and accountability in language testing in the context of 'alternative assessment', as well as a critical discussion of its possibilities and limits.

■■■

BERNARD SPOLSKY: *Measured Words*. Oxford University Press 1995 (*see* Text 18)

The first half of the book is a history of language testing; the second provides a meticulously documented history of the introduction of the TOEFL test and its capture by the testing establishment, and is a fine example of the new discipline of critical language testing.

■■☐

ELANA SHOHAMY: 'Critical language testing and beyond' in *Studies in Education*, 1998 (*see* Text 19)

This landmark paper represents the culmination of a number of years of original work by Shohamy, drawing attention to the implications for language assessment of the writings of Foucault on tests and the growth of critical applied linguistics.

Chapter 8
New directions—and dilemmas?

■■□

MICHELINE CHALHOUB-DEVILLE (ed.): *Issues in Computer Adaptive Tests of Reading Proficiency*. University of Cambridge 1999

This collection of papers examines the development of the new area of computer-adaptive tests of reading comprehension from a variety of theoretical, practical, and technical perspectives.

■□□

HAROLD S. MADSEN: 'Computer-adaptive testing of listening and reading comprehension' in Patricia Dunkel (ed.): *Computer-Assisted Language Learning and Testing: Research Issues and Practice*. Newbury House 1991 (*see* Text 20)

This paper provides a useful introductory discussion of issues in the design of computer-adaptive tests of language.

■■■

T. F. McNAMARA: 'Interaction' in second language performance assessment: Whose performance?' in *Applied Linguistics* 18/4, 1997

This is a critique of current orthodoxy in language testing in the light of views (adopted from discourse analysis) of the intrinsically social character of second language performance.

SECTION 4
Glossary

Page references to Section I, Survey, are given at the end of each entry.

accountability A requirement of language tests, that they be answerable to the interests and needs of those taking them. [72]

achievement tests Tests which aim to establish what has been learned in a course of instruction. [6]

alternative assessment A movement for the reform of school-based assessment, away from standardized multiple choice tests and towards assessments which are more sensitive to the goals of the curriculum. Typically includes portfolio assessment, exhibitions, records of participation in classroom activities, etc. [7]

analytic rating The **rating** of each aspect of a performance separately, as for example (in writing) grammar, organization, content, etc. [43]

authenticity The degree to which **test materials** and test conditions succeed in replicating those in the target use situation. [9]

classification analysis A procedure for establishing the degree of agreement between different **raters** when categorizing performances in terms of a **rating scale**. [58]

cloze test A test of reading in which a passage is presented with words regularly deleted; the reader's task is to supply the missing words. [15]

competency A specific practical skill used in the planning and assessment of adult training outcomes. [69]

computer adaptive test A test consisting of a bank of items; as items are answered further items are selected which will most contribute to the emerging picture of the candidate's ability. The test thereby adapts itself to each individual candidate. [65]

computer based testing (**CBT**) Procedures for presenting test material (stimulus and task **prompt**) via computer to candidates, who respond using the computer keyboard. [79]

consequential validity The way in which the implementation of a test can affect the interpretability of test scores; the practical consequences of the introduction of a test. [53]

construct irrelevant variance Differences in the performance of candidates on a test which are unrelated to the ability or skill being measured. [53]

construct under-representation The failure of a test to adequately capture the complexity of the communicative demands of the **criterion**; oversimplification of the construct. [53]

constructed response formats In test questions, formats which require the candidates to generate a response in their own words, as in **short answer questions**, and performance on tests of speaking and writing. [30]

content validity The extent to which the test appropriately samples from the **domain** of knowledge and skills relevant to performance in the **criterion**. [51]

correlation coefficient A **statistic** summarizing the extent to which one set of measures (e.g. of weight) is predictable from knowledge of another set of measures for the same individuals (e.g. height). [57]

criterion 1 The **domain** of behaviour relevant to test design. **2** An aspect of performance which is evaluated in test scoring, e.g. fluency, accuracy etc. [7]

criterion-referenced measurement An approach to measurement in which performances are compared to one or more descriptions of minimally adequate performance at a given level. [62]

critical language testing An intellectual movement to expose the (frequently covert) social and political role of language tests. [72]

cut-point (also **cut-score**) The point on a scoring continuum at which a classification decision is made; e.g. whether a candidate has 'passed' or 'failed'. [38]

data matrix A set of scores used in **psychometric** analysis of the qualities of a test. [56]

direct testing An approach to testing which emphasizes the need for close simulation of the **criterion** in the test. In the testing of speaking, the **Oral Proficiency Interview (OPI)** is a **direct testing** technique. [8]

discrete point testing An approach to the development of tests in which tests typically contain multiple items, each of which focuses on a single point of knowledge, e.g. of grammar or vocabulary. [14]

domain The area of knowledge or skill or the set of tasks constituting **criterion** performance, and which is the target of the test. [25]

ethical language testing A position advanced within the field of language test development and research to ensure that their practices are ethical and socially responsible. [72]

face validity The extent to which a test meets the expectations of those involved in its use, e.g. administrators, teachers, candidates and test score users; the acceptability of a test to its **stakeholders**. [50]

fixed response format In test questions, a method for candidates to record a response which requires them to choose between presented alternatives rather than constructing a response themselves. [5]

high stakes tests Tests which provide information on the basis of which significant decisions are made about candidates, e.g. admission to courses of study, or to work settings. [48]

holistic rating The **rating** of a performance as a whole. [43]

International English Language Testing System (**IELTS**) A performance based test of English for academic purposes, used mainly for the selection of international students at universities in the United Kingdom, Australia and elsewhere. [24]

impact The total effect of a test on the educational process and on the wider community. [72]

integrative tests Tests which integrate knowledge of various components of language systems and an ability to produce and interpret language appropriately in context; seen as a necessary complement to discrete point tests. [15]

inter-rater reliability The extent to which pairs of **raters** agree; technically a **statistic** expressing degree to which the **ratings** of one **rater** are predictable from the **ratings** of another, based on the **ratings** given by each for a given set of test performances. [58]

item analysis Procedures for investigating properties of **test items** (especially difficulty and discrimination) prior to development of their final format and content. [60]

item bank A set of **items** which have been developed and **trialled**, and whose **psychometric** properties are known, which can be drawn upon in the development of individual tests. [80]

item difficulty The relative difficulty of a test item for a given group of test-takers; the proportion of candidates getting a particular test item wrong; cf. **item facility**. [60]

item discrimination The extent to which an individual **test item** distinguishes between test candidates; the degree to which an **item** provides information about candidates which is consistent with information provided by other items in the same test. [60]

item facility The relative ease of a **test item** for a given group of test-takers; the proportion of candidates getting a given test item correct; cf. **item difficulty**. [60]

Item Response Theory (IRT) An approach to measurement which uses complex statistical modelling of test performance data to make powerful generalizations about item characteristics, the relation of items to candidate ability, and about the overall quality of tests. [64]

job analysis The work of identifying tasks and roles in the **criterion** setting which can be used as the basis for task design in **performance tests**, particularly in specific purpose contexts. [17]

level descriptors In **rating scales**, statements describing the character of a minimally acceptable performance at a given level. [40]

moderation The process of reconciling or reducing differences in the judgements and standards used by different **raters** within a **rating procedure**, usually at meetings of **raters** at which performances at relevant levels are rated independently and then discussed. [44]

multiple choice format A format for test questions in which candidates have to choose from a number of presented alternatives, only one of which is correct. [5]

norm-referenced measurement An approach to measurement in which an individual performance is evaluated against the range of performances typical of a population of similar individuals. [62]

normal distribution A graph in the shape of a bell-shaped curve representing the frequency of occurrence of values of typical measurements in biology and other fields; the known statistical properties of this distribution are used in the interpretation of test scores in **norm-referenced measurement.** [63]

operational version The final product of test development; the version of the test which, following improvement through **trialling**, will be used in actual test administrations. [60]

Oral Proficiency Interview (**OPI**) Popular format for the assessment of speaking skills in which the candidate engages in a directed interaction with an interlocutor; developed for the US Government in the 1950s, and influential in many contexts since. [23]

paper-and-pencil language tests A traditional test format, with test paper and answer sheet. [5]

performance tests In language tests, a class of test in which assessment is carried out in a context where the candidate is involved in an act of communication. [5]

pilot version A version of a test written during the test development process which is to be tried out, and its material subsequently revised before use in actual test administrations. [60]

pragmatic tests A class of tests identified in the work of Oller which meet his requirement of pragmatic naturalness: essentially, that the language user's grammar be engaged in contextual production or interpretation of language under the normal constraints (including real time processing) of communication. [15]

proficiency tests Tests which aim to establish a candidate's readiness for a particular communicative role, e.g. in a work or educational setting. [6]

prompt In the assessment of speaking or writing, the stimulus to which the candidate responds in speaking or writing. [31]

psychometrics The science of measurement of individual cognitive abilities, involving the technical, statistical analysis of quantitative data from test performances. Adjective: **psychometric**. [14]

Rasch measurement A branch of **Item Response Theory (IRT)**, named after a Danish mathematician; particularly useful in rater-mediated testing environments, as it allows investigation of the impact of rater characteristics and task characteristics on scores. [65]

raters Those who judge performances in productive tests of speaking and writing, using an agreed **rating procedure** and criteria in so doing. [6]

rating procedure Agreed procedure followed by **raters** in judging the quality of performances, particularly in the assessment of speaking and writing. [6]

rating scale An ordered set of descriptions of typical performances in terms of their quality, used by **raters** in **rating procedures**. [40]

ratings Assessments of performance, recorded as scores on a **rating scale**. [35]

reliability Consistency of measurement of individuals by a test, usually expressed in a **reliability coefficient**. [61]

reliability coefficient A **statistic**, usually on a scale from 0 to 1, expressing the extent to which individuals have been measured consistently by a test. [58]

response format The way in which candidates are required to respond to **test materials**, e.g. by choosing from alternative responses (**fixed response format**) or by writing or speaking (**constructed response format**). [26]

rubric The instructions to candidates before each question or task. [31]

self-assessment The process by which learners are trained to evaluate their own performances, e.g. imagining how well they would cope in a range of real-life settings. [7]

semi-direct test A test of communication in which there is some compromise in the simulation of real world communicative activity; e.g., in a test of speaking, where the **prompt** is presented via tape, and the candidate speaks not to another person, but records his/her response on a machine or computer. [82]

short answer questions In the testing of comprehension, items which require candidates to express briefly what they have understood in their own words. [30]

skills testing The testing of the four macroskills (reading, writing, listening, and speaking), usually done separately from one another. [14]

stakeholders Those who have an interest in the development and operation of a test; e.g., funding authorities, educators, test developers, candidates, receiving institutions, etc. [50]

statistic A single number summarizing a set of mathematical relations within data, e.g. within scores from a test administration. [57]

test construct What is being measured by the test; those aspects of the candidate's underlying knowledge or skill which are the target of measurement in a test. [13]

test content What a test contains in terms of texts, tasks, item types, skills tested, etc. [25]

test development committee A formal grouping of major **stakeholders** in a test development project, who supervise and respond to the progress of the work and advise on policy and practical matters. [73]

test equating The statistical process of demonstrating the equivalence or at least the exact psychometric relation of two versions of a test, particularly how difficult they are. [64]

test items Individual questions or tasks faced by test -takers. [5]

test linking Establishing the relative difficulty of different but related tests; can be used to measure the growth of individuals over time. [64]

test materials Texts, tasks and questions to be used in the test. [00]

test method The way in which the candidate is asked to engage with the materials and tasks in the test, and how their response will be scored. [25]

test security The need for candidates not to become aware of the specific content of **test materials** before the administration of the test. [24]

test specifications A detailed accounting of the test format and general test design which serves as a basis for providing information for candidates and test users, and for writing new versions of a test. [31]

test-taker feedback The opinions of test-takers, usually at the stage of **trialling**, on the content and format of **test materials**; used to revise the materials. [32]

test users' handbook (manual) A book prepared by those responsible for a test, giving information to candidates and score users about the content and format of the test, and on how to interpret scores and reports on test performance. [73]

test validation The process of investigating the quality of test-based inferences, often in order to improve this basis and hence the quality of the test. [10]

The Test of English as a Foreign Language (TOEFL) A test of English as a foreign language used to assist in the selection of international students wishing to study at American univer-sities, developed and administered by the **Educational Testing Service**. [24]

trialling (also **trying out**) The process of administering pilot **test materials** to samples of subjects representative of the final test population, in order to gather empirical data on the effectiveness of the proposed materials, and to enable their revision. (Verb: to **trial**, to **try out**; noun a **trial**, a **try-out**). [32]

Unitary Competence Hypothesis The idea that a number of superficially different test types, which however meet the requirements of **pragmatic tests**, all depend on access to a single capacity for the production and interpretation of language in context, and are therefore, in a sense, substitutable one for the other; particularly associated with the work of John Oller. [15]

validity The relationship between evidence from test performance and the inferences about candidates' capacity to perform in the **criterion** that are drawn from that evidence. [9]

washback The effect of a test on the teaching and learning leading up to it. [72]